COURTNEY M.

A Mother's Loss,
A Daughter's Legacy

PATRICIA BRUSHA
COURTNEY ELIZABETH MICHAELS

Copyright 2021 by Patricia Brusha

ISBN: 978-1-7379984-0-2

Library of Congress Control Number: 2021920922

Published by Purse-Impressions
Cave Creek, AZ 85331

First Printing October 2021

Printed in the United States

Dedication

To my best friend, twin, and love of my life,
My beautiful daughter Courtney.
I miss you every day!

TABLE OF CONTENTS

INTRODUCTION

The first few days after Courtney passed away were a blur. I was fortunate to be surrounded by my family and close friends, but I was in shock. I couldn't comprehend that I had lost my 28-year-old daughter.

I was numb, angry, in denial, sad, and I couldn't believe this was happening. Courtney was my everything. We were twins; a mini-me and the best of friends. We didn't just talk every day but multiple times a day.

We had the same laugh, loud voice, and similar ways of thinking. We sincerely enjoyed each other's friendship. I could not, and still can't two years later, accept that I could live my life without her in it.

My husband, my stepkids, my sister, my niece, my friends, and Courtney's friends were there to support me through the toughest days of my life! When her two best friends, Kelsey and Sam, asked me if I wanted them to retrieve Courtney's things from her apartment, I immediately said yes. I couldn't bring myself to go to that apartment and pack up her few possessions. When they returned, Sam handed me Courtney's journal and said with quiet reverence, "I kept this separate as I thought you might want it."

I held the journal close to my chest and thanked her for bringing it to me. It was a black BING notebook I had gotten from my friend at Microsoft. It was now tattered. When I quickly glanced at it, I noticed it was filled with words, phone numbers, doodles, and pieces of paper.

It scared me to read it, yet I hoped it might provide me with some answers. I wasn't ready to confront it, so I placed it on the windowsill next to my bed where it sat for over a year. I knew in my heart there would come a day when I would open the cover and discover what was written on those pages.

Ironically, I had kept a journal of my own, documenting the details of Courtney's tragic illness and her final days.

I started writing my journal on Mother's Day, 2019. I knew in my gut it would be the last Mother's Day we would have together. What I didn't know is she would be gone only a few weeks later.

Shortly before her 2-year *Angel-versary* (June 4th), I opened Courtney's journal. Two things immediately became apparent. The first was how much we think and write alike and how similar we are in style and tone. I wasn't sure if it came from all the times I helped Courtney with her writing or if it was genetic. Either way, I had forgotten the similarities, and this was a bittersweet reminder.

As I read the words, I could hear her voice inside my head. It was like I was listening to her talk. I had missed hearing her, and the journal gave me an instant connection back to her.

Secondly, the story wasn't scary at all! It was about a girl who had lost the love of her life to an overdose; a girl who desperately wanted to beat her addiction; who wished for a better life, and who was trying to cope with her grief.

After reading it, I thought her words might help inspire others. Courtney's intent was to publish her journal, but that's not all she wanted. She didn't like the fact that women who graduated from rehab often left with their personal items in a plastic bag. So, she came up with the idea of giving purses to rehab graduates, and that is how Purse-Impressions came to be, but more on that later. Now, on with the story.

Part One of *Courtney M.* is her initial journey through rehab in 2015.

Part Two is my journal of her last days; a story about a mother losing her daughter.

Part Three is the birth of Purse-Impressions, the charity inspired by Courtney's idea.

My hope in sharing this book is that it:

- ♥ Brings people hope and inspiration.
- ♥ Allows for conversations about alcohol and substance abuse to come out into the open.
- ♥ Honors the life of my daughter so those who loved her remember her amazing spirit!

For those who didn't know her, I invite you to become acquainted with the sweet soul, loving daughter, great friend, and kind person Courtney was.

This is Courtney M.

PART ONE
COURTNEY'S JOURNAL

This Journal is dedicated to you: D xxoo

"God grant me the serenity
to accept the things I cannot change
The courage to change the things I can
and the wisdom to know the difference"

Life Inside Rehab

Wednesday, 1st of April, 2015

This is no April Fool's joke. I FINALLY got released from detox jail and have moved to the treatment side of the rehab house! :) The road to recovery officially begins. I walked through the doors and started the next part of my journey with a tour given by Lee, a blonde chick who did my intake originally. She said she was happy to see me, and my face lit up.

Lee showed me to my room, "3" where I will have a roommate named Ash. I unpack the few items I have (in comparison to her stuff) into a small drawer. I then put out my stuffed animals, all frogs (including my best stuffy, Bertel) on this much more comfortable (pillow included) bed. Towels are provided and there's even a damn window, which I can see out of.

I got water in the cafe here, and after 5 pm we get to watch TV. I'm sure it will be odd when it comes to who chooses what to watch with so many people here, but I am still excited because I didn't see or hear any fun noise during the days I was in detox.

Next, I sat in the meetings room to look at the sun, which I hadn't seen while I was in detox either. The phone on the wall, old school, rings twice in a row, both times for me! POPULAR! I can start having visitors tomorrow.

Thank God, maybe they'll bring me some outside food! I'm craving beef jerky and chips. I am so going to get fat. I also need deodorant; it wasn't on my list of what to bring to detox. My mind was on trying to escape my current situation, finally giving in, and answering yes to going.

Today, at 4 pm, I am allowed to go outside!!!! Then, dinner at 4:30 pm like old folks, and 7:30 pm a Cocaine Anonymous meeting. I'm a little scared, but I've got D's coin on me and his AA book under my new pillow.

First thing that happens is the group phone starts ringing off the hook. First Jord, next Jerry, then Big Daddy (my stepdad who cried), and AR (my ex-husband). I caught everyone up on my changing sides from detox to rehab, and it seems everyone is super supportive.

I got to go outside and go to 7eleven. Bought myself Lays Dill Pickle Chips, beef jerky, and some soda. I'm going to live off sugar and fats! This evening at dinner, I met my roomie, Ash. She is 18 and has been here 3 weeks.

Going to my first CA (Cocaine Anonymous) meeting. I have heard it can be very emotional and a possible trigger. We'll have to find out, I guess. Another girl I met on the detox side gave me $5 for chocolate bars. I CHANGED into new clothes and am going to clean my clothes tonight. I smell like sweat.

Lunch - Chicken cold cuts, salad, vegetable soup and buttercups

Dinner - Rice pasta, Caesar salad

Snack - Cake, which I couldn't eat because I am celiac

First TV show we watched was *Etalk Canada*, and I got to know some of the girls:

Ash F. - 32, two kids, homeless, on disability, her 3rd time. Going to the big rehab house after this week.

Meg - 30, nearly died from an overdose and had to come back here to detox/rehab and then a 3-month program.

Ash (roommate) 18, escort, stripper, crack, meth, boyfriend in jail, has until Sunday and then moves to the other house.

Lee - 40, 9-year-old kid, divorced, crackhead, 3rd time here, been in jail over 3 years.

Some things I learned at CA tonight:

1. Do it for you.
2. The why's will go away.
3. When you finally let in the possibility of change and take the same drive you had and use it to "get" on your health/recovery, things will turn around.
4. Addicts don't drink for a reason; they drink due to addiction.

Stayed up watching *The Client* with Ash and Lee. Had soda, ate chips, and stayed up until 2 am after lights out to hang out with Ash, laughing in bed. Just enjoying making a new friend.

How am I feeling?

Loved, Anxious, Lonely, Proud
Withdrawn, Exhausted, Confident
Annoyed, Optimistic, Confused, Hopeful
Angry, Excited, Disappointed, Aggressive
Relieved, Thankful, Happy, Frustrated,
Alienated, Satisfied, Scared, Tired, Guilty
Determined, Ecstatic, Depressed, Energetic
Upset, Overwhelmed, Undecided, Peaceful

I made it through my first day out of detox!

Triggers

Thursday, 2nd of April, 2015

Slept through the night but slept in sweat. I had to change my clothes twice. Up at 7 am, as we heard a knock on the door. I was first to shower and then headed down to find out my duty is garbage and lunch. Went to Timmie's (Tim Hortons Coffee), got an icecap, and then texted a few people. I am waiting to hear about visiting hours.

What I learned at my meetings today:

1. You need something to control when you give up the control of holding booze in hand or drugs.

2. Be grateful, remind yourself to be grateful and pass it on.

3. Remember last night & GET up at 7 am

4. Practice recovery. Like the way of bed making, peace, neat, and nice.

Breakfast - Rice Krispies
Lunch - Broccoli soup & salad

Dinner - Chicken, potatoes, green beans
Snack - Sandwich and veggies

Program 1-2 PM Meditation/Scrapbooking
How I am feeling: Triggered

I am uncomfortable with meditation; it scares me, and I don't like feeling vulnerable. So, it was suggested I do an activity instead, like scrapbooking.

I can understand that it's better to keep busy than doing nothing at all, but scrapbooking makes me feel like using at this moment. I relate to scrapbooking as getting high and going into the comfortable routine of focusing on doing another line of coke and pouring another drink.

I want to try it, but it makes me scared it will be a trigger. It could be helpful to open up with photos and such, but then I see/feel old feelings. I feel awkward seeing scissors on the table and magazines. Like, really? Magazines means we are forced to scrapbook from media which, for me, represents the physical and mental acceptance of drugs, alcohol, and smoking.

I think I will stick to writing to fill my time in between meetings and chores.

Realization! Maybe D gave me his Big Book not only to help me release my pain, but also to help me grieve his death. Maybe he realized he was not going to make it!

He called me the night he died and asked me to hang out with him. I said I couldn't, but we could do it tomorrow. Apparently, he decided to go out with another friend. This so-called friend brought heroin, or something with him, and D slipped up and overdosed.

The guy dumped his body in a snowbank and left him there. He was just down the street from the sober living house where he lived. Someone spotted the body in the morning, and I got the text when I was out to lunch with my mom.

I miss him so much my heart aches. I have his book and all his coins. I know he would be proud of me. I got the visiting hours schedule for Friday through Monday, and I already have company booked. Got to make sure I have eyelash glue.

Tomorrow will be Austria

Good Friday, April 3rd, 2015
Baby Sophia's 1-year B-day

Last night, the five ladies walked down Dundas to Bathurst Street, past "Honest Ed's" and grabbed Timmie's and got rained on. The roads seemed busy on our way to our first outdoor AA meeting with a group of 40+ women. We socialized over coffee, which, btw, the amount of caffeine I'm drinking is more than I've had since giving up coke (soda) over 3 years ago, and I was NEVER a coffee drinker.

The event was okay. Lee and I discovered we had met at a conference before. The meeting was just like every other thing, always the same, but I opened my mind and listened to what they were saying. I had a realization and burst into tears.

Last night, I had to sleep in the observation room because of an allergy attack. You see, I have Celiac's disease, meaning I can't eat any wheat, and I am also allergic to eggs and soy. I got to sleep in because of the holiday, but then at breakfast, the weekend staff were real bitches. They didn't allow us to have outside food. They totally forced me to eat their food, yelled at others, and changed the lunch time schedule. Then, my 'lunch' was a head of lettuce and a fucking pack of turkey cold cuts!

I feel so disrespected. Dinner was pasta salad and mayo sandwiches with deep-fried fish and two stuffed mini peppers on the side, which were soy, wheat, and egg filled.

So, she gave me carrots and broccoli. That isn't a fucking meal! All I can eat is damn chips, chocolate, and soda. Completely going to get fucking fat! Plus, so unhealthy.

AR (my ex) came from 4 pm-5:30 pm to catch up and attempt to keep me mentally sober. I was totally losing it today!

6:00 PM Positive Thinking Group
·   Self-talk can affect how you do in here
·   Build Your House of Self-Esteem
·   Remember texting miscommunication
INTERNAL
·   Denial
·   Guilt / shame
·   Depression
·   Physical appearance
·   Personality

- Psychological
- Trust

EXTERNAL

- What others think
- Media
- School
- Religion
- Abuse mental/physical
- Drugs & alcohol
  - Post-Acute Withdrawal Symptoms (PAWS)
  - Happy calm reactions in brain
  - Tired, excited, forgetful
  - Headaches
  - Substance - need to readjust
  - Chemistry – 18 - 24 months to recover
  - Do this =feel this

After the meeting, I spoke to my case manager. I have to wait until Monday to get the mental okay from the hospital. Then they will give me the date for when they can move me to the next house! This place is a holding area after detox while we wait for beds to open up in the big house.

I spoke to Jerry and the girls, my two besties, BFFs, today for the first time. So, that was quite a treat! We bitched and laughed with sober craziness.

There are 11 of us here now and tons of crazy.

Everyone wants to leave, go, or stay. I'm the kook with D's book with my numbers in it and my journal attached to my hip.

Everyone is starting to get on each other's nerves. I showed a girl the card game Kings in the Corner, and in turn got chocolates for my generosity. The ladies who work at the intake even thanked me for allowing them to view the magazines my mom brought me.

Dinner was another fucking wreck. It was deep-fried fish and pasta salad, and the only thing they had for me was Goddamn veggies the size of my palm.

All my girls in the house had a meeting of basic bitching about the food I was being served. Missy was standing up for me, and Ash had to buy me chili in order for me to eat. This is complete B.S.

Not only are we losing it, but we are also just miserable. I spoke to Jerry, and, of course, he's out at the bar with Kes & G. It was a complete trigger, and I yelled at him and hung up! I did say sorry before going to bed but only sorry for going to bed angry!

They didn't even fucking care about my recovery or give me verbal support as much as it bothers me; NOT. AR always says thank you and how much he is proud of me. I spoke to AR and DB (my cousin), and they will be visiting me tomorrow. We watched Fried Green Tomatoes and went to bed around 12:30 am.

One time when I was 19, I went on a Con tiki tour of Europe, where I met AR, and I totally partied my ass off in Amsterdam. I was so sick, I thought I'd be hung over for the entire rest of the trip. But the next day, we woke up in Austria, and it was beautiful, and life was good.

So, my mom and I came up with this saying: "When a day is bad, just wait, "Tomorrow will be Austria!"

I Want to Live

Saturday, April 4th, 2015

I slept through the night without a pee break or sweating like a crazy person. I woke up around 10 am to some eggs and toast, so I didn't eat anything except Rice Krispies.

Today is a two-hour outside visit! We all got primmed and proper with showers. I put on new eyelashes and even conditioner on my hair. I used the bathroom hand dryer to dry my hair and borrowed a straightener! :)

Looking sexy and clean. I used a razor to do my armpits. They make us send back the used ones to throw away. Guess some people use them for bad things.

At lunch, I heard a woman had a seizure outside smoking today and got picked up by an ambulance. On top of that, Missy, my crackhead friend who left and came back, got discharged. I hope she stays clean. I got her #.

It looks like rain. We are all quiet and looking at magazines my mom brought. I labeled them 1-6. So far, 2 are already missing They seriously weren't kidding, "Here for yourself, not to make friends, & don't trust a soul/addict."

They say we will go outside today; it is already 12:30 pm, and I haven't got time for that as I won't miss a moment with my 2 pm-4 pm event/catch-up/ sober day out. Ash may come as well. We may get a piercing for the hell of it! Why not? If I am staying here and staying sober, I need to have some fun.

We had a lovely time out and funny enough, Ash admitted to me she finds DB sexy. I hear that, as I have before, from the entire crowd of ladies after he and AR leave. He is VERY good looking, but, dude, he's my cousin. LOL!

One of the funniest memories of the visit is when DB and AR showed up, after the ladies had gone to the dog park for air in my mom's green beetle. We grouped into the small car and went to lunch, and I ate STEAK!!! It was delicious and the most food I've eaten in the past week.

I am so full, like legit, I'm the fattest I've ever been. Chips, soda, and chocolate is absolutely not healthy nor helping me stay at a good weight. We went to Ardennes and AR bought me 2 shirts, 2 pants, and 4 of those tote bags I like, the ones you buy as a gift with purchase.

We came back on time and listened to music and

danced in the parking lot. DB said, "Turn down the music before everyone is dying to get into rehab because it looks like so much fun!" LOL

Dinner came, and I had a reheated piece of chicken, eww. I spent the rest of the evening talking to Jord on the phone, laughing for an hour!

I also heard from my mom. We chatted about detox, lockdown, food, the hobo who shit herself here, and my issues with staff and food.

She was understanding regarding my thoughts about day programs and my mental health recovery. I want to keep up my treatment after I get out of this hell hole, in case I have to wait to get into the longer rehab program after this.

Look at me, saying the word rehab all casual. I am honestly not worried about the other rehab place anymore. I just need to have my mental state completely together for me to keep up with recovery.

As I write this, all I think of is D's last piece of writing, the one I found in his little pieces-of-paper box. It said:

"I Want To Live!"

Crazy for You!

Sunday Funday
EASTER!!!

I woke up this morning with a call from my bestie, Kelso! She wanted to wish me Happy Easter and tell me about a party she went to last night. She's off to her boyfriend's family event this afternoon. I then spent time listening to her.

Clare and I went to "church" today. It was snowing and cold as hell. Wish it was possible for global warming to actually fucking come and create the proper weather, called Spring, on April 5th.

I got to paint my nails and did Ash's eyelashes. Her first time EVER?!!, even for being a working girl. I guess I'm just vain, always having my hair blonde, even having extensions, and always, always having eyelashes on!

There have been so many things going missing around here like food, clothes, and personal belongings. They are going to do a search. I am completely down for this as I'm confident in how I am following the rules.

2 pm rolled around quite quickly today and so did my lovely period :(That sucks.

Jord picked me up, and we enjoyed one another's company as we went to lunch and caught up. He looks incredible as ever. I told him I couldn't believe this was my 5th day in rehab after detox and it was actually going pretty well. I said I have even been enjoying the meetings. Our visit went fast, but I was happy he came to see me.

Dinner tonight will be a traditional Easter dinner. Luckily, Kel is working (a celiac herself) and had gotten me a breakfast of tomato, bacon, and cheese.

I feel bad, but I yelled at Jerry a lot today and hung up on him three times. I think I'm feeling upset that he gets to do things and I'm missing out, especially regarding MY life and MY friends.

AR and Jord have their own lives, and it doesn't bother me to hear about their drinking or partying. But the minute Jerry tells me about his stuff, I get so angry, like he's living my life! Jealous, that is what I am. Wow, that was a shock to discover and admit.

I miss D, he'd understand and know exactly what advice to give me.

After writing this out, I chose to call and talk it out/apologize to Jerry. He said he will come visit tomorrow.

For Easter dinner, we ate ham, broccoli, chickpeas,

mashed potatoes, and apple pie...all homemade. I ate so much I felt like a big fatty!

Still buzzing from a sugar rush, we watched 13 Going on 30! That is one of my all-time favorite movies. I think about watching it with my mom and us dancing to the music in the movie.

Lots of bickering with the house crazies who weren't into the same film choices, but it worked out. I ended up staying up last to watch the end with Ash. I was bawling my eyes out at the end when he gives her the dollhouse back.

That's my picket fence house! We were so jazzed up from the movie we took Tylenol Nighttime to sleep through. I went to bed still crying and singing "Crazy for You" ...this time the tears were for D.

Forty-four Days

Monday, April 6th, 2015

Another holiday in Canada...Easter Monday

Happy Easter Monday. Last day for us to enjoy a day to sleep in. Got up around 9:30 am and had the morning meeting. L & I signed up for the dinner dishes, and I hopped out to the cab to Dr. T's office. I had help with the directions, and, luckily, I was able to arrive on time.

I got signed in, and they gave me a piece of information that mentioned me getting a shot for TB and having to get tested.

I'm losing my shit; I absolutely hate needles. I am petrified of them!

As I wait, this woman in the waiting room asks me about my drug of choice, and I somewhat casually answer. Then she goes on about HER opioid addiction. She's on day 13 of 35, and she doesn't think she will make it. I could care less about her; I am having an anxiety attack waiting for the shot!

I thank God for Jerry today. He came to my rescue on speaker phone to calm me down while I was getting my blood work done. "You'll be okay," and, "I know you can do it." He kept repeating as I squeezed my eyes shut. God, I hate needles.

I got back and had some time to read and chat with the girls. We all got ready for the 6:30 AA meeting and my irritability started to kick in!

Monday AA Meeting
"Give it your all for a year."
"If you hate it, go back out."
"90 in 90, Sponsor, Home Group"
"What do I want to do today vs. when/ where/ how can I get a drink?"
"Do it to feel. Don't wait until you want to. You'll learn to do/want it."
"Do into feeling..."
"It's a moment in time"
"A design to living sober"
"Grateful vs. Proud of you"
"Acceptance=the table is yellow, call a spade a spade, and forgive everyone else for their sickness"
"Asking Why won't be answered. It's What am I going to do with it?"

After the meeting, (which was an open meeting), Jerry, me, Ash, and Lee ran some errands before finding a pub to eat at. Lee ordered fish and chips and she got a hair in her food. The waitress made her another one and then continued to charge her the full amount.

Jerry tried to be nice and ordered a non-alcoholic beverage. When he asked for chocolate milk, she rolled her eyes and said, "Well, this is a pub." Bitch. We didn't tip her more than a dollar.

When we arrived back, Jerry bought me some snacks. He used money from his rent savings to pay for things for me. He dropped them off, and oddly, he left while I ran upstairs to drop off my jacket. I felt so bad not being able to say good-bye or thank you.

SE (one of my guy friends) called me on his break from the shelter and told me how proud he was of me! He said my experience in the house sounds like the shelter he was at. LOL He also said if I want to do any sober activities when I get out of here, he would be down for it! He said he'd even come visit me.

I spoke to my mom as well which made my day! We laughed away about everything going on here and how much she loves being back in Arizona. She seems quite happy and super-supportive. She said she can come visit me Thursday when she is back in town.

My day was also surprisingly blessed with a phone call from my big sister. She called me to give me advice, support, and tell me how proud of me she is. I love my sister. Hearing her voice and her cute American accent made me feel so at home. It's the way she says she loves me; tells me I've got her support, AND us going over the experiences she had.

She advises me to stay strong, keep it up, and that she knows I can definitely make it through. "You should be proud, honey, you are doing this at the right time. This is the perfect time. I love you so much."

Taking time to enjoy the evening, I keep thinking about D. I've got his socks on. I hate socks! But he is always here, all around me, keeping me warm, keeping me sober.

Ash and I watched *Starsky & Hutch* while bitching to Lee as she did her word searches. I love how she jumps up when she can't find a word and hands it to Ash and me to find it, makes me crack up! What a ham!

Dinner was such bullshit. I don't even remember it already. Dessert was even worse, chips and popcorn. Side note: Char didn't clean up as her duty, and she barely did the laundry; just dumped it on the floor, so it had to be redone.

It was major jokes night. A cross between sugar rush and nut house, we all ended up dressing like rappers. Ash had her new "fat butt" jiggling around in the stupid pants she got from the clothes donated to the house. She was so funny!

We also enjoyed our squats and calf raises and stayed up until 2:30 am just blabbing. She showed me some of her man's writing and his upcoming court info.

I lay in bed last night and the night before wishing for the confidence and strength to stay until my official release date. The final date after both houses would be May 12, 2015, and I would be 44 days sober.

D made it 44 days on the day he relapsed and died from an overdose.

In These 5 Minutes

Tuesday, April 7, 2015

I don't want to relapse, nor am I feeling the urge to drink or want to relapse. I just want the pain and the mental why's to have answers. There isn't a feeling to drink other than for social purposes as in, "Let's go for coffee," which in my experience, usually ends up meaning, "Let's go for a drink!" Yes, I know you can surround yourself with people who would actually mean coffee when they say, "a drink." I legit am so proud at this moment to say I am enjoying my sobriety. I'm so happy and proud that I am NOT doing drugs anymore, that is for sure. I just wonder why I had the urge to substitute drugs with drinking.

But in these 5 minutes...I'm okay.

Whenever everything was going good, Big Daddy, my stepdad, would always say, "In these 5 minutes, everything is okay."

I don't see a need or want for drinking. Fuck, I quit drugs alone before I came here, so I can only imagine with support how amazing I can do; how I can prosper in taking down this addiction and the mental abuse I put on myself.

I love me today!

Guess who got a notebook identical to mine, minus being leather and free! Shadow! She sits in each room that I am in to write, looking over at me to see if I'm writing. Then she straps it up and carries it around to show people. She's such a copycat.

She's disappeared tons of times today. We are starting to get suspicious she is jacking our things. It all adds up now. Shadow needs a bra. A bra goes missing. Shadow arrived with only one pair of socks. Socks go missing. Shadow is hungry, but always eats candy which she buys with only $10???

I feel bad because she is just a young girl, but I worry about how she will end up because she keeps trying to be rebellious.

I went to light therapy today! I am so proud! I am so embarrassed by my psoriasis. I got clearance today, finally, so I jumped into a cab and booted over to the women's college hospital.

I ran into my nurse and explained the odd circumstances that have affected me and why I have not been able to attend light therapy.

1. Deaths 2. Distance 3. Detox...AKA the three D's.

On D, again there it is, he is on my mind and my heart. I know without those things he left me I would not have had the courage to go through detox. Literally,

I don't think I would have been pushed over the edge enough, with my "everything happens for a reason" mindset, to get myself up that morning and make that call without his coin in my hand, his book in my lap, and my froggy cuddled tight.

9 days later, I am sitting here clean. Sober. I got back from light therapy to have lunch which ended up being sandwiches and soup I couldn't eat. Maria, the cook, gave me attitude about asking what soup broth she used, which indeed had wheat flour listed as the second ingredient. I had to eat...guess...lettuce and tomatoes again!

Ash turned 32 today, and we got her a "sober bunny". I got her a $10 Tim Hortons card and a card signed by all of us. She LOVED it and couldn't stop thanking us. She said we made her birthday incredible!

I got my hospital card today, so I can go without any other paperwork to get acupuncture. A tiny, little Asian woman walks me to a darkened room and shoves five skinny needles into each of my ears. Then I meditate while soft music plays in the background.

I can't wait to talk to AR and tell him I meditated today!

The experience sparked something good and bad all at the same time. I breathed deep. I felt pain in my ears, but I also felt the pain release, and my pain was gone. No more pain.

This reminded me of D, in peace because he is no

longer in pain, but feeling hopeless he is gone forever. Nothing left, no feeling; not just being without pain. I remind myself as I meditate, pain is only temporary.

Then a number popped into my head as I walked back (the girls were getting smokes), and I dial the number. There it is. His voice. D! His gorgeous, fresh, healthy, happy voice talking to me. His voicemail giving an update on where to call him. My eyes start to water, and my heart speeds up.

D, the love of my life, the reason I'm here recovering; 9 days sober!

I dialed his number over and over, just to hear his voice.

God, do I miss him beyond belief. My heart aches.

Everyone got sick this evening and started throwing up. It ends up only four of us, (2 of the new house guests here on supportive stay), make it to the Narcotics Anonymous (NA) meeting this evening.

Let's just put it this way, I wasn't impressed with the speaker. She never mentioned her DOC (drug of choice) but just referred to her addiction. She mentioned how she wished over and over that when she was alone in the alley or in the washroom using that she'd just die alone, leaving everyone to suffer without her knowing.

I got up and left. I burst into tears. I could play the guessing game, but by now it should be obvious who came down after me. Not for support, but to say she was having a hard time listening to the speaker as well. Shadow!

The meeting finally ended, thank the Lord, and I got to speak to AR and tell him all about my feelings and my experience. He brought up the example of the "Dump Truck" going past you on a highway. You get the choice to allow it to pass like waves...up and down and flowing versus jumping on your surfboard and riding on that wave until it crashes against the shore, taking you down with it.

I lay in bed with D's AA coins in my hand, pressed against my heart, with my stuffed frogs surrounding me. The rain starts pouring down, and I hear it crashing on our window. I hear sick housemates throwing up all around the house.

I clutch D's AA book and hope everyone is better by the morning. Tomorrow will be day 10 sober.

I can do this. I am strong; therefore, I shall be a healthier person.

Hump Day

April 8, 2015

Boundaries-Divine Divas
    3:00-4:30 pm
    1) Spirituality
    2) Emotional Wellness
    3) Psychological
    4) Social
    5) Physical

All 5 of these together equals equilibrium; without one or more, your life is out of sync!
GUESS WHAT DAY IT IS??? Hump Day!
Iggy Azalea is playing in my head, "Work, work, run up sorry, but Ramona let's put this in the past. It's just that the bitch kept staring so I had to whoop that ass."
I'm on my way to the morning meeting after getting up four times to go to the washroom overnight. Every time I headed back to bed, I'd press D's coins to

my heart. Everyone is exhausted for some reason. It could be the pouring rain and gloomy skies, which I live for, or it could be the major sickness that has been going around the house. Ash & L threw up all night long. :(Poor girlies.

Another day, another copycat. I mean, I don't want to spend all my entries on my Shadow, but I want to document this and show how this is evolving into a full-on obsession. She now has a tote bag she carries around, crop top, socks (too big on her like D's socks I'm wearing), boots, and her journal attached to her hip!

AR says I should be flattered. I'm just annoyed! I like being me/different/unique. This is one busy day, but I have good news. It hit me that it's hump day, and I've made it halfway through the week already. I've got only two days before the visitor weekend.

I'll have my mom and AR, and maybe the girls and one of the family members come by. Two hours each day out, plus possible visitation in the lounge.

Then, it will be the last week of my stay here; I've got my intake date at the other house. I'm feeling positive, just nervous about not having ANY communication with the outside world at the next house. I will be allowed two visitations, and one of them is when my big sister comes up to Canada with my niece May 8, 9, 10th.

I can do this! I can make it in the next place, even though it sounds harder and more intense. I also heard you get a ceremony, or graduation of sorts, when you make it to 21 days. Ash and some of the other girls will be there at the new house with me. See ya, Shadow, ha-ha.

Anyways, I'm on my way to light therapy for the second day in a row, and I'm taking the streetcar all alone! I went over to Frank's Restaurant and ate soup and drank Dad's Root Beer alone. I texted AR, and he said I'm back to me, more of myself. Alone, reflective, happy, and independent.

The rain continues to pour, so I head back, walking to the streetcar with my hood off and my smile larger than ever. Got back in time to get into a disagreement with the in-house cook, Maria, over her not reading the actual ingredients and getting flustered about feeding me. She thinks I'm just being picky.

So, I went right to the woman who runs the place instead. She was super-supportive, and she got me a pass for my mom to bring food, so I can eat what is more accommodating to my celiac condition.

Next, we went to acupuncture, and I enjoyed it again. Really getting into it; relaxing and so enjoyable overall. Its free through the Ontario Health Plan for addicts. So, I am hoping to continue it when I'm out.

Afterwards, we had Divine Divas at TWH and there were two women speaking about socializing and getting out there again now that they are sober. The one woman I just wanted to hug.

In the afternoon, we had a social worker come and

do art therapy. They asked us to close our eyes and picture what we wanted for ourselves, then draw it.

This is the odd thing...I drew that white-picket-fence image I've had in my head since I was 13!! I really enjoyed drawing and finger painting while sober. It was fun! I didn't even realize I was doing something I never thought I could do sober. Then I thought about it, and I was so excited!

Look at me being able to do art without drugs.

Dual Recovery Meeting
Halt
One day at a time
Believe
Pay attention
Don't give up
Honesty
Remember when
Gratitude
Keep it simple
This too shall pass
Breathe
Trust
How important is it
Easy does it
Patience
YOU ARE NOT ALONE!

"Today I believe there is a reason we go back to meetings."

"Work, work, work."

"When you don't put your recovery first, your attitude changes or you take on too much stuff."

"Learn to unlearn things. Don't wait for a 911 call."

"I don't want to hurt myself anymore - medication, drugs, drinking, not speaking out."

"The world is your playground once you get clean."

"Start to feel comfortable being uncomfortable."

"My worst day sober is better than my best day drunk."

"You are not alone. But that's exactly what I want, to be alone with my addiction."

"Making my unmanageable life manageable."

The last meeting of the evening was CA (Cocaine Anonymous). We had an incredible speaker. She spoke about how from seven years old until forty-three she used coke/crack and alcohol and then turned to escorting. Married and then divorced, now her best friend in her life is her ex-husband. She really felt like a real person.

I am so proud of her! Recovery is within reach! :) :)

Mom

Thursday, April 9th, 2015

During the morning check-in, I relayed my excitement to see her for all to hear. Quick update: Deni is getting her craft on and making my mom a thank-you card with a necklace made from magazine paper.

She cuts magazine pages into long triangular strips. Then she tightly rolls them onto a toothpick, glues them, and varnishes them with nail polish! Then she strings them together to form a beautiful piece of jewelry.

Today is also Ash F's last day before treatment. I plan on speaking to my mother and AR about when I should discharge before entering the full treatment center. I plan on going home to conquer a list of things such as car insurance, taxes, laundry, and, of course, grocery shopping. I mustn't forget to have unlimited cuddles with all the fuzz children.

AR has sent me some incredible pictures of our cats, Pumpkin and Sedona, laying in the laundry basket and just being adorable cuddle monsters!

Off to double recovery, and Shadow has turned into a complete bitch, or maybe you could call it childish behavior. Two new chicks moved over this morning from detox, and by the end of the break, they both disappeared.

Jerry is visiting me today, and we're going for a walk. I messaged D's sister, and, oddly, I got the message she is going to detox at the mental ward of the hospital. She said, "D would be proud of me." She mentioned she can see him smiling at me with pride. That just made me feel so good and so proud!

Shadow spent the day stealing things and being rude to everyone in the house. I'm so over it. Please, Lord, just come and give our house some peace. The house is still a sick mess, and everyone is just miserable. I feel like a horrible writer today. Been so reflective, yet distracted, and I'm just keeping tabs on what's going on, but my mind keeps racing to write out all my thoughts.

Too many meetings, so little time. Chris, aka "Towel" has now moved into our room. It is pouring rain again, and she enjoys the rain as much as I do. Lee and I did laundry, and my boots and winter jacket are finally clean. But, the jeans, dress (night dress), and underwear are all ruined due to the crusty washing machines here!

Mom is here!!

My mom brought me to Tim Hortons and gave me

a bracelet she also has that says BELIEVE! This reminds me of the stress ball I gave her I got in therapy that said, "Believe in Yourself."

When she came to visit, she donated food, notebooks, and pens to the house. The whole house was all over that. Deni is being so creative, as usual, and created my mom a sobriety necklace.

My mom spent about an hour here, and I enjoyed (using that word again) talking and catching up. Man, I'm getting lazy with my vocabulary.

My mom took my photo, and it was cute when everyone asked where my psoriasis spots had gone because they barely showed up in the photo she sent out.

Recovery Meeting 5:30-8:00 PM
"When does it stop?'
"Leave Regret City."
"You cannot change anything."
"Pick up the pieces and start again."
"Responding versus Reacting!"

I'M FEELING UPSIDE DOWN AT THE MOMENT

Fallen Addicts

Friday, April 10th, 2015

I woke up in an incredible mood. Whether it was from the beautiful rainstorm or not, I slept the entire night through without the sweats or being woken up. Maybe it was from seeing my mom and falling asleep on a full belly without just sugar and chips; just real cheese, meat sticks, and a slice of gluten-free bread my mom brought.

I got breakfast today!!! First day I had three whole meals that filled me so proper and tasted so good. I thanked the cook, Maria, a ton and overall lost my temptation to just eat junk and chocolate. For breakfast, I had toast, with real butter and honey (thanks, Mom). Lunch, which I was able to fit in for once, was a turkey and salami sandwich and mushroom soup.

Finally, a delicious dinner of baked fish, mashed potatoes, and even some steamed vegetables.

During the morning meeting with the girls, the ones I live with plus two new ones, Kel, the meeting leader, mentioned some problems. Bedroom Three has clothes piled up in it and looks messy. Our new roomie apologized and went to fix it.

Next, she mentioned Room 4, Bed 2, Shadow's!! She explains the bed isn't made there. Shadow starts the lying, blaming others, and overall whining. My blood starts to boil.

I had woken up happy, and here starts the childishness already. I stand up and go get ready for light therapy and hear yelling in the hall on the phone.

Shadow is yelling at her father who is on his way to visit. She is telling him not to come look for her and says she is going to go use again and it's his fault. She slams the door behind her.

What an ungrateful child! I swear I was bad, but only to myself. I was evil or missing but never a whining brat.

Jump forward to me walking back from therapy to our house/detox/shelter, whatever you call it, and there are the cops out front.

As I pass Mel, the house manager who is speaking to the cops, (here you can "Cue the Higher Power Moment!" and not lose your shit) a car pulls into the spot, and it is Shadow's dad. His phone had been off, so I guess she was yelling at his voicemail, and he didn't get her message. I brought him over to introduce him to Mel and the cops.

We all explained our versions of the story. Oddly enough, Mel took the address Shadow had written down and copied it herself. An older man in his mid-40's picked her up to grab drugs and have sex with her. Her dad didn't seem surprised at all and even thought he knew who the guy was.

Shadow's dad went to grab her things and filed out a form that allowed the cops to issue a warrant for her breaking her probation. Now they can find her and bring her to a hearing or a mental ward at a hospital since she is still under 18. How disappointing to come through treatment and then just give up.

Sadly, I knew she wouldn't make it. Each day we get better, stronger, faster, less withdrawn, and more positive; Shadow's emotions get worse each day.

All the best to our fallen addicts!

I walked inside just in time to hear everyone's opinions about things that went missing when Shadow left. I met up with our little crew, and we headed over to acupuncture. I placed my earbuds in, so whenever I felt pain, I would just push them deeper inside my ears and try to meditate through it.

Jerry came to visit me but had missed the train twice, don't even ask, and only arrived in time to sit with me for 20 minutes. He told me he had "no plans" for the evening but kept asking me about mine, which is somewhat amusing since they are the same every day: wake up, meeting, self-time, meeting, eat, eat more, self-time, meetings, repeat.

So, I come to find out he dips out of here to go see some chick he failed to mention. That really pissed me off. Thank God I was able to speak to AR on the phone and vent my feelings. I swear he was high on catnip, he made me laugh. We chatted until I went to my room and caught up with the girls.

What a day!

ZZZZZZZZZZZZZZZZ!

8:00 PM-9:00 PM

Public AA Meeting

"Forget what you should remember and remember what you should forget!"

"Service keeps you sober."

"It's not about timing, it's about what you are actually doing toward recovery."

"I see what you are going to become."

"Meeting makers make it."

"At age 14, I was told I drank what the other alcoholics (in the room) spilled."

"I jumped off an 8-ft.-story building and lived!"

"You can't run away from yourself. There you are!"

"They were people with whacko stories like mine, and they all had huge smiles on their faces."

"What do I have to lose? What if I try?"

"Make an apology and clear the air."

"One big pink cloud when you take it in!"

"Luck, coincidence, impossible...GOD!"

"Today I have a life better than I could have ever dreamed!"

Movie of My Life

Sunday, April 12, 2015
Lee (40) and Dem (28) Birthdays

AA Meeting 11:00 AM-12:00 PM
    At this meeting, we got to see Ash receive her 1-month chip! Congrats! Lee turned 40 today and received her desire chip for another 24 hours on her b-day!
    "When I put alcohol in my system, I want more."
    "I didn't know I had a problem because everyone around me could drink like me, or more!"
    "I'd remember the one good time and always drink trying to get back to that time."
    "I resented him for drinking (5 years older than me) but went right alongside him always blaming him for the reason I continued to drink."
    "Blame it on the moon."
    "I thought I could just leave all my pain behind."
    "Always negotiating with my mental obsession to drink."

"If I wasn't depressed, I'd be able to drink normally."

<u>"Just not drink today versus giving it up forever."</u>

I finally got it! Just ONE day at a time. The compulsion is totally lifted from me today. Replace the urge with another thing to do.

I wonder what my story is. How would it sound?

Tomorrow will be here before I know it. Like, gosh, today is day 14. At my worst, I could never imagine ever making it on a car ride to or from a job or going to lunch without the possibility of a drink.

My addiction prevented me from doing things or going anywhere without alcohol. What gave me fear (this is no excuse) was going someplace that didn't serve alcohol, so the option was no longer there for me to say no, even though, in complete honesty, why would I say no? It was more like a self-brag for me to say no, like I had to prove to others and myself that I could be strong enough to say no. As if I was in control! Ha-ha-ha-ha!

Look at me now, I've gone to multiple (4) lunch dates at pubs, and I am satisfied without booze. I realize if the server doesn't say 'alcoholic' drink, that I don't even have it in mind. I even encourage others to go drink whatever because it won't affect me.

I get to see Jord today, which I am quite excited about! I want to show him the "desire chip" since he told me on the phone the other day, he has gone a few days without drinking. I legit would NEVER think I'd say or actually feel proud of him for doing so. Selfishly, it gave me an excuse in the past to drink if he did too. I love his efforts and soul.

People come into your life for a reason, and even having him around now is such a blessing.

I know one of the AA steps is to clear the air and work on mending past issues/situations, but I don't want that to be the only reason/push/etc. to amend my faults. I am sober now, and I'm truly sorry. I appreciate him and all we had and anything we might have in the future.

But I am living for today, and today I'm grateful to be in his presence! I think it's called unconditional love. I still want to push him in his wheelchair when he is old! LOL

First Viewing Meeting
8:00 PM- 9:00 PM
"I was born an alcoholic waiting for my first drink."

"Tuesday is an in/out day at the rehab. Only 2 out of 10 make it."

"Aftercare for the family."

"You didn't fail, you've already succeeded by making this conscious decision."

"No matter how long you've been sober, just look at today."

"Dealing with it, you change your friends to start

a new journey."

"My heart is pumping but I'm not scared."

"JUST FUNCTION!!"

"It's easier to run away and start fresh than it is to fix what's already broken!"

"You are braver than you think/believe, stronger than you seem, and smarter than you think."

"Life is full of things you didn't think you could do until you did them."

"Get through the day without hurting others or hurting yourself."

"Opportunities are in my eyesight, it's me who says yes or no to them. It takes courage."

"Growth is painful, literally!"

"Liquor Store says "Fresh Start" - what the fuck!?"

"It's none of their business, and I don't care what people think about me."

"'Thanks for sharing' versus telling people how stupid they sound; move on."

"For me not to care is impossible, I am an alcoholic!"

After Jord picked me up in his big, black truck, the two of us had a cute cuddle to greet one another. I look up to see the girls banging on the window yelling and screaming, "You Go Girl!"

We got the chance to drive to Queen Street to the first Carl's Junior in Canada. I got a lettuce-wrapped hamburger. Jord and I got the chance to catch up, and he gave me some support I truly needed. Especially from him.

He is a star in my universe, and when it shines bright, I feel like my sky is within reach!

Absolutely an incredible two hours spending time together. After our chats, I came back to the house feeling like I was able to breathe fresh air. I am so lucky to have some unique people in my life who secretly push me further on my path to clean up my current life situation. All just by being there, listening, and speaking to me honestly. I gave Jord the 24-hour desire to be sober chip I got for him at the meeting this morning. I realized for who, and why, all AA/CA/NA meetings start and end with the serenity prayer. I like that they say, "Let's take a moment of silence for our fellow alcoholics inside and outside these walls."

They asked about anyone who has the desire to be sober in the past 24 hours. Jord came to mind since he told me about his cutting back. Sidenote: I envy, in the nicest of ways, how he can do it on his own without support, and I got him his first-and-only desire chip.

The gorgeous smile that shot across his face when I gave it to him and explained what it was, made my day. Hopefully, yes, I am hopeful today, it will help him with his own journey.

Dinner was made up of hotdogs and beans, which were delicious. Jen, who has been 1-month sober and is here on a supportive stay before a 6-month program, asked Cor and I if we'd like to come to an AA meeting at the new house I will be transferring over to shortly. My next steps.

I was like, "Hell, yes!" We walked through China-town to get there and got to see the area, shops, and the rehab house, which, as Jen said, will be her stomping grounds "for the next 21 days on the road to the rest of my life." Excitement came over me, and I even got butterflies as we walked up the steps....

Inside the house, I saw a couple of girls who had been in the current house with me. They told me the horrible news that one of the girls we all knew relapsed and got kicked out of the house. She had breathing problems and went to the hospital where she had a tracheotomy at age 29! This is quite sad.

In my future writings, when I get transferred to this house, I'm sure my feelings about the place will continue to change, but as for my overall first impression, I'm excited. It's very homey and reminds me of the movie Running with Scissors.

It's about a few people living with a psychiatrist who has his office in his house. He supports the kids doing 'crazy' things to express their minds and find themselves.

In the new place, everyone gets their own hotel-looking room, which scares me a little. I find comfort in others being around even if we aren't in constant communication.

I'm not alluding to any fact that I can't or don't find ease in being alone, but I like to know there is someone/something present. I know this must stem from issues from my childhood.

Another memory, which has haunted me since the beginning, is how my mother was robbed (I was 14) the night of my confirmation and how eerie the house felt after that; bars being put up on the windows and cops questioning me as if I did it! Not to mention, scraping off the footprints from the wall in the basement and seeing fingerprints on the staircase railing.

Ironically, the best thing ever (silver lining) was after the robbery we got Cabo, a Wheaton Terrier, a fluffy cloud with the biggest heart and best personality. My mom, Big Daddy, and I went to pick out a puppy after the robbery, and we knew right away he was the one. He was such a presence and in our family for 10 years.

Mine and AR's cats, Pumpkin and Sedona, have literally saved our relationship and kept AR out of depression. I got them for him, secretly, but also for me, indirectly.

I have come to realize how I kept feeling horrible about how our marriage crumbled right away due to me being my addict self, my immaturity (would never want to admit that out loud), and the fact that I chose partying over the life I've so desired.

I found pain deep in my heart seeing him hurt, which I ran away from accepting, but it forever ate at my soul. My Soul. He truly is my soulmate, no matter what that means. His smile, laugh, and overall happiness since I brought home those kitties makes my heart beat with joy. Thank you, Shannon, for the cats!

I arrived back to the oddest news and the first time Cor has opened up or even SPOKE! Her daughter came to visit and had some news to give her. She had said how proud she is of her mom for going into detox and getting treatment for her alcoholism. Her daughter is 21 and she is pregnant, due in 10 days, and she has had a boyfriend for 5 years that she had never mentioned to Cor. The reason she kept it a secret was that she fears her brother's reaction because her boyfriend is black. She (Cor) will now be a grandmother. How exciting! This place continues to amuse me with its characters, and I feel like I'm in some odd movie of my life....

Narcotics Anonymous meeting
6:15 -7:15 PM
"We create versions of ourselves for others."
"Every time I live alone without anyone around to give me normality, I mismanage."
"I never shared, just thought about my dirty secrets alone."
"I'd start losing track of time, and I OD'd."
"How would I ever get to 18 months?"
"Told them about my problem and continued to use."
"You are not a loser; when you walk in, these people here are all going through the same shit."
"Find someone to call who gets what you're going

through."

"No shame and no guilt every day."

"Give it 10 minutes, and it will go away."

"It's a festival of feelings, being an addict."

"It's a mental obsession not a physical craving."

It is Ash's last night sleeping here before her smoking-hot addictions counselor picks her up to go to the new house. We are helping her pack up. Ash gave me a piggyback ride up the stairs like a monkey, then we got yelled at about it.

4 am rolls around, and I wake up to see Ash wide awake. She is nervous about moving to the next house, and I am sad. We sit in the dark hugging.

Changes

Monday, April 13th, 2015

MONDAY ROLLS AROUND AGAIN!

Fifteen days in, and I'm feeling incredible!

My horoscope today (my birthday is January 7, 1991):

Capricorn Dec 22-Jan 19

Persistence and determination can unlock doors. Patience is required, or you can try again later. In a disagreement about priorities, fulfill financial obligations. Do what you said without losing your temper.

I am more scared of losing friends than being afraid others will leave me. I know I need to walk away. It's like I must leave others because it's healthy. The old me used to go out of my way to be there no matter what, even if it was bad for me.

AA Meeting

"The three P's: people, places, playgrounds. This will help set boundaries, and as one goes, the new people

will come through fellowship and respect those boundaries."

"Wherever I go, there I am!"

"You're on a bridge over the water, you're on fire.
Would you jump in or question why?"

"Long live the rose that grew from the concrete
when no one else cared."

We barely slept. Got up around 6:30 am to help
Ash prepare and get some food before she leaves and
moves to the next house. She gave me a sweater I am
ever so fond of, a pair of lumberjack jeans, and, of
course, she tried to force me (friendly) to wear socks
she bought! (I never wear socks, only D's).

We distributed her extra toiletries to the women in
the house and detox who may have come with nothing.
I plan to keep that tradition up as I feel it's a way to
give back.

I will miss her.

Due to the lack of seriousness the cooks have taken
regarding my food allergies, I decided to fill out two
formal complaints.

CLIENT COMPLAINT FORM

This form is to be used for clients for the purpose of
documenting a complaint involving a staff member. The
record of information should be nonjudgmental and will
be signed off by the client. The completed report will
then be forwarded to the Coordinator of the Center and a
copy sent to the manager.

Date: April 10-14

Client Name: Courtney M.

Details: This is an overall complaint regarding two staff members, S & T, for whom the list of specific events would take up multiple pages. I have never been so disturbed, mistreated, demoralized by human beings who have chosen as a career to be in social working; working with marginalized populations. Specifically, the tone in their voice, their feeding off one another (which is highly unprofessional), them bringing up personal life situations, and comparing multiple individuals in the house.

We are asked to respect rules and not trigger others to the best of our abilities: this should be respected by staff.

CLIENT COMPLAINT FORM

This form is to be used for clients for the purpose of documenting a complaint involving a staff member. The record of information should be nonjudgmental and will be signed off by the client. The completed report will then be forwarded to the Coordinator of the Center and a copy sent to the manager.

Date: April 12th 5 PM

Client Name: Courtney M

Details: Due to severe food allergies, which have been noted and documented prior, it was made clear foods be checked in each meal for gluten, soy, or eggs.

The cook did not explain what was in the food, and I threw up immediately in a trash bin. She walked off yelling from the stairs, extremely insensitively, "Do you need your epi pen or something?" Then walked off. She did not acknowledge or address the issue.

K politely asked for me to be monitored for 45 minutes to keep an eye out for any reaction. Then, at 6:15 (I missed break), I asked the cook if I could make myself something to eat as I was hungry, and she replied, "I'm off duty, so don't ask me for help!" The next cook, whose shift hadn't even started, made me dinner.

I met Ashley's addiction management worker who is super-supportive even though he doesn't know me. What a sweetheart. Maybe he is single - ha-ha - or a potential sponsor. He works for Ford and mentions they'll have programs for jobs and support groups.

As soon as Ash leaves, I feel completely alone. This is a first. I just feel like I am the last one left of this group of women, with all its ups and downs, to be waiting for treatment in the big house.

This afternoon, both Mel (who is heading home) and Suz (who is new - I don't really know her) are leaving! This means there will only be a total of 5 ladies in the house!!

It's quiet already, minus, of course, my loud voice which makes up for like 5 people on its own. Cor, Deni, and I are heading to acupuncture, where I'm actually going to do meditation. If this is what AR describes, I'll listen to the sound of waves from the cd player, and I'll breathe in with the wind and out with the wave, in with the wind and out with the wave....

Breathing exercises are the opposite of my addict brain, which is never calm but always "alone" because it thinks differently than the average person.

But maybe I am not alone. Maybe there are other addicts out there who can relate to the steps along the way of my journey.

Fresh Air

Friday, April 17, 2015

As I sit down in the salon chair to get my out-of-detox house-and off-to-rehab house hairdo done, I tell the hairdresser all about my adventures so far; how this came about because of the deaths (D and Uncle M) in my life; how it sparked the rollercoaster of my life to peek to the top and head straight downhill.

He was supportive of me and my story. His other client, a nurse who was waiting for her hair to process, just looked at me sympathetically. She told me how incredible it is that I took this step!

As my hairdresser gets to blow drying my hair, he starts to describe D, without me saying a word. He mentions the time D brought me to get my hair done at the old salon. He described his neck tattoos, the romantic relationship we showed for each other, and how we had booze on us. I'm pretty sure we were doing blow too, oh, Lord!

This was one of the first 'remember when's' I've

experienced. My eyes water as I miss my lovely D.

"You are like a gecko. You change your color to fit your background instead of showing your true colors."

AA 8:00-9:00 PM

"Saying I don't know can be freeing."

"Have a drink then a hangover - the problem continues to rise."

"You don't have to continue your day in a funk."

"Guilt is that you've done something, shame is that you are something."

"We are lucky to come here versus poor me."

"I have a defect of character, not defective."

"You can always do more."

"You don't go looking for a Cadillac in a junk yard."

"After you've completed step 9, the promises come true."

"Say sorry once, good for you, say sorry twice, that is not okay. Say sorry three times for the same behavior, that's bullshit!!!"

"Resentments will kill you if you don't lay them to rest."

How could I keep breaking my parents' hearts? My stepdad is not blood-related, but it makes me hurt putting him through all of this.

F.E.A.R

False Evidence Appearing Real

or

Fucked-Up Emotions Appearing Real

or

Face Everything and Recover

Today my mother supported me by attending an AA meeting. She said she found all alcoholics in the meeting LOOKED different than she expected. I wonder if our outside image has changed since AA, or if we just never looked in a mirror while intoxicated to see how bad we looked.

Daily reflection meeting 12:15-1:15 PM

"I don't want to be at arm's length for a drink, I want to be twelve steps!"

"What I resist will persist."

"AA is like McDonalds; you find consistency and the exact same order anywhere!"

Walk Away

Tuesday, April 21, 2015

Welcome to The New House I'm in bed #7. (my favorite number).

I would like to start off this entry with an apology. I'm sorry for not writing as frequently, as I enjoy it. The days since Monday, April 13th, when Ash left the last house and came here, were filled with many post-detox experiences.

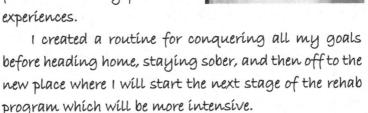

I created a routine for conquering all my goals before heading home, staying sober, and then off to the new place where I will start the next stage of the rehab program which will be more intensive.

I had planned to do a thorough recap of the last days before leaving the old house, but each day I slept in feeling like I had no purpose or friends I wanted to hang with or go along with on their 7 am smoke break.

Kris had moved into my room, and we hit it off quite well. She is such a character; the cutest thing who makes me laugh with her quirkiness. She laughs at me like I'm a comedian, ha-ha.

Breakfast had finally become manageable as the cook got the hang of my celiac and provided me with my bread, cheese, meat, and some fresh fruit. :) I also took the time to use my crude "how-to-take-the-street-car map" that Mel had made up for me.

I used the streetcar to get to light therapy, meet up with some of the girls to go to acupuncture, meditate, and then go to the daily afternoon AA meeting. After that, I was able to have guests between 4-5pm and take a billion notes at the meetings that evening.

The thoughts coming from my sobering mind were racing, and I had to talk out the emotions or they would disappear before I could grab my pen and notebook. So many realizations came through the dark clouds of the sky, but I could not see the stars just by the moonlight.

Each day, my check-in had more joy, excitement, realization, and happiness to it. This AA step/action/notion is just incredible, to say the least. I feel real again. "In these 5 minutes...everything was okay." (Big Daddy's saying)

My clothing style got weirder (like back 5 years ago), my eyes wider with joy, a cuter pep in my step, more outgoing with my personality, and much more insightful. Meetings became what I wanted to do; I looked forward to them.

A sense of loneliness and reality was forefront in my mind. During these days, Cor opened up to me, and there is one moment I shall never forget. She came to sit in the pouring rain with me as she shared her story of drug abuse and alcoholism.

I couldn't believe what a fox she had been and bad ass, kicking the shit out of her husband, not to mention how she got him thrown in jail for starting a crack house.

I finally got in touch with OW and got a meeting set up for Thursday, which means I will be breaking out of here one day early by a few hours. This will allow me to get to the other end of the city to get money from the government to help while I work on stabilizing my life during this trying time.

Deni made me the most beautiful lime green necklace with a frog on it. RIBBIT!! It made my day. That evening, during my usual soda run, Gol unleashed the devil and got in a huge argument with Deni and started throwing things at her.

I ran to the house manager as I was getting scared. I was horrified I'd see Gol hurt poor Deni who was yelling, swearing, and slamming things around. I'd honestly never thought I'd see that from Deni.

I finally wrote the formal complaints against the workers and got lucky enough to go into the donation room with Kristina. We had a competition to see who could get the ugliest outfit from there and wear it to an AA meeting. Ha-ha.

I continued to speak with my sister, which always made my day shine brighter. Jerry came to see me as well, and we found a new spot at the dog park down the road to eat my new addiction: jalapeno beef jerky and soda.

Our friendship, or whatever relationship, has continued to crumble, and he has turned on the guilt and anger to the point where I now just hang up. I went to a stress management class which is good because my "reaction" to stress or anger is bad for my recovery.

My psoriasis, and ultimately my long-term health, is what my 'walk away' tattoos on my calves now mean to me. It used to mean "fuck you," but now it means walk away from my addiction.

The feeling of leaving the first house so abruptly is playing Jekyll and Hyde with my mind and current emotions.

My bubble of safety from outside influences, even though it drives me nuts, (all the scheduled/mandatory consistency and support) is about to pop. I now have to decide if I genuinely want recovery because need seems to play a different role at this time of my life.

I NEED recovery, but do I want it enough to work, work, work?

Going home, I have a goal to go to meetings, see my family, see if I can visit friends without booze, and kiss those damn fuzzy dogs right on the lips!

I miss AR and the old times when he would pick me up at the airport. He would always have his hair cut and his room clean; meaning he would shove everything in his wardrobe.

I just feel like he will be understanding and help support me during my mental confusion when I step outside this bubble of sobriety and bring it into my life and home.

I am sure Bryer and Cabo are incredibly fuzzy, and I'll get to see the cats, Sedona and Pumpkin. So excited :)

Sound Bytes

Wednesday, April 22, 2015

First Meeting Day
  9:25 am -11:30 pm
  "Addicted to adrenaline and fast-paced life = chaos!"
  "Goes nuts on sugar to fill in the blanks."
  "Productive member of society and can continue 12 steps to fill the void."
  "Happy vs. Buzzed!"
  "Maybe anxiety isn't there; every time you talk it out, you feel better."
  "A meeting is like an allergy shot."
  "Any negative chatter in your head: remember what you learned in week 1."
  "One drink on a patio leads to wasted in a gutter."
  "Being sober is like your skin is too tight."
  1. Denial + Isolation
  2. Anger
  3. Bargaining

4. Depression

5. Acceptance

Topic Meeting 2-3 PM

"Once I accept, I can no longer use that as an excuse."

"It's not the outside world that needs to change, it's me!"

"Acknowledge vs. acceptance!"

"Denying denial!"

"As well as we can manipulate others, we are good at manipulating ourselves

"Drugs and alcohol are not the problem; they are just a coping mechanism for deep-down issues

1. Always have a beverage

2. Don't confuse thirsty

3. Leave if you need to

"I just must have something in my hand. Does that mean I want to fit in? Is that it?"

"Until now, our lives have been devoted to running from pain and problems. We fled from them like a plague. We never wanted to deal with the reality of suffering. Escaping via the bottle was always our solution. Character building through suffering might be alright for saints, but it certainly didn't appeal to us."

"They say we are selfish people, then they say to take this time to completely focus on ourselves. Isn't that contradictory? Letting our higher power take care of it, but what if he doesn't?"

"Your job is recovery!"

"When I stopped living in the problem and began living in the answer, the problem went away."

"Alcoholism is like backward glasses."

"A 5-year-old is more in the moment and aware of what's needed than those of us who are using."

I'm braindead ATM

Group Meetings

April 23, 2015

This afternoon was absolute bullshit talking about keeping the house clean, which is just logical. We are addicts, not idiots! So, I don't get it.

I was told writing is not good, and it has upset me. This may not work for others, but it is the only thing keeping me sane!

Group meetings 2:20-4:00 pm
Twenty-four hours a day in my book
"For the next reader - stay strong! It will be hard, your urges will overpower you, but have faith in yourself."

"It's possible, even for someone who struggles as much as you do!"

"My mind is like a bad neighborhood, never go there alone."

I haven't really talked at all in the new house. I'm

listening, but everyone is told to be selfish here, so who do I open up to???

"I couldn't stop vs. I didn't want to."

"They can't understand when something tragic happens in my life because I'm strong."

"When in doubt, do what's hardest; the most difficult path is invariably the right one."

"I question myself, yes, but I don't live without compassion for myself. If I didn't love myself, why would I be here?"

"Be your own best friend, not your enemy!"

Family

Saturday, April 25, 2015

I know I am writing more sporadically, but that is due to time constraints: the reading, the self-discovery, the meetings, bedtimes; I find it a bit difficult to put all my thoughts and experiences onto paper fast enough.

TODAY IS THE BEST DAY EVER! MEL CAME AND BROUGHT ME A FROG! He is dark green with white and black eyes, spiky hairdo, and white feet just like my cat, Sedona. I am over the moon. Today, I woke up on the good side of the bed.

I just had my first family visit, and I'm feeling inspired, sad, and homesick. I just feel like curling up in my bed and snuggling with my frogs and my journal in silence. I feel withdrawn from the house at the moment.

Everything couldn't have been more perfect. When I arrived back to my room, alone, where I sit now, I opened the cards from my mom and Big Daddy, telling me how proud they are-DAY27! Then, I looked at a bright yellow envelope which read "Maple."

I already feel those warm, salty tears come to my eyes I have not felt since the first few days in detox or at that AA meeting in the rain at House #1.

To my heart's delight, there it is, a "pumpkin" cat card with the most beautiful words written inside. My lovely AR, pudding as I call him, has written me. Funny thing, he still hasn't gotten my card and doesn't know that what we both said to each other, oddly enough, is so similar.

The pure fact that he got me a card, wrote it, used my nickname (we gave each other nicknames 5 years ago while writing back and forth across the fucking world) is just perfect!

My heart is filled with love beyond any words. He hugged me and said I'll see him next weekend. I can't wait. I feel like dialing his number already. I truly know he is going through his stuff, and I may never have the right words to say to him, but I cherish our relationship.

I love AR, he is my best friend. He said to focus on me, and he'll take care of everything else, our fuzz children and all.

Feeling Sad

Monday, April 27, 2015

We write our own script in life, then we publish it to help others. I need to do the steps. D had his goals and started on his steps. Okay, then get started on those steps!

I miss you today, D!

I don't know what to do with the feeling of sadness. This is when I would run away from these feelings by using.

I need to talk to a counselor today; it's minutes prior to the end of class, and I have burst into tears!

You need to hear your story once and move forward with all these full days of discovery and looking into ourselves. I feel like I could go on and sit in silence with myself. Yes, me, myself. I don't want it to disappear like in the past. I just feel like I'm healthy and emptied of all the squirrels running around in my head.

Now I can go breathe, take a bath, and read a book.

Could this mean I have found peace rather than numbness?

Work, Work, Work

April 28, 2015

Congratulations 30!

Big Daddy always says, "in these five minutes" and get a good night's sleep. There must be a higher power as he mentioned.

Rupert the Frog is the coziest in my arm.

If it doesn't hurt enough, it doesn't get our attention. I feel that I am breaking the cycle! Am I going to do the work or not?

I do not want to drink again. Oh, I want to live; to have this recovered life, focused, I'm happy...work, work, work!

"Honesty to self."

The Package

April 29, 2015

Today, I had my seven-day review, on day eight, at the new house. B and I went through my workbook, and we investigated the possibility of me being a perfectionist. This could be part of why my life took its downward spiral of alcoholism; I wasn't having perfection.

As I write, I think back to my failed relationship with AR, my family, and not getting what I expected of my relationship with J.

This was the time my drinking became more significant. When I drank, I thought things were better than they were.

I thought of drinking instead of just changing jobs, boyfriends, or friends. I didn't admit to myself that part of me, deep down inside, was not completely happy. I was so in love with the idea of my white picket fence that I sacrificed my own happiness.

I would go out of my way for others to make them

happy because I wanted perfection. I spoke with the counselor about me being stubborn, and how I didn't finish school because I couldn't get perfect grades. I couldn't have the perfect marriage, so I left!

100% or nothing! That's how I lived my life!!

I also touched upon the grief I was feeling and suggested I should set up another one-on-one session to learn tools specifically for this area. I want to make sure I'm in the best mental place possible so that I won't relapse after treatment.

Already in a down mood, the evening counselor came to my room and asked me to come to the office after dinner.

I see it, a FedEx envelope that I must open in front of them to check for drugs or anything harmful. My poor eyes and my soul! The first thing I see is a note I had written to D the night before heading to rehab.

I go through the four stapled 8 by 11 pieces of paper and start feeling overwhelming pain before getting to the actual notes.

What the fuck is this? The lady at the desk asked me if this is a joke? Is this a murder scene?

I burst into tears, ran to get Bertel, and continued to go through the package. Someone had written a drunk note describing how they went out of their way to desecrate D's gravesite. Then they felt bad, due to AA, and went back to the site to make amends. They wrote they will amend me later with photos showing their attempt at making amends.

I want to make sure whoever sent this keeps away from me forever as they they've hurt me badly already.

I look into my stuffed frog Bertel's eyes, and he is so innocent; he loves me and is so cuddly. Frightened, angry, and scared, I call my mom. She is with JJ, my confidante and close friend, in Arizona down by the pool. Interesting! Thank you, higher power, thank you.

My mom listened to the story, and JJ said he's going to mail me a letter and to hang in there. I need to conquer this disruption and travel to Arizona when I get out. I need to do this grief healing without any intoxication. I need to call AR and continue writing a letter I started to D's mom.

Who did this? Why did this happen? Only me! Only today! Thank you, Bertel, for being here.

Keep Your Walls Up

April 30, 2015

I'm terminally unique and more vulnerable than I thought since gaining sobriety. I gave my last name and address to others hoping to get mail and forgot it's supposed to be anonymous. This protects us, and I allowed myself to be found without realizing it. This may be the reason for changing phone numbers, deleting emails, etc. Just wish I hadn't given in so quickly.

Keep your walls up, Courtney!

You need to be aware of the amount you share starting now, otherwise the same journey you took down you'll be taking back up.

12:40 p.m. Another letter. Another fucking letter from this GG guy. I wait until after my lunch, which was delicious on the bright side, to open it and see red letters across the page with no rhyme or reason.

It is filled with derogatory words that even I am too embarrassed to write here, and photos from the crime scene where D was found. I run to the office when

I realize he has named in the letter the exact woman, Sana, who is here today. He used the head office of the rehab as the return address. Creepy.

DB, a counselor here, has asked me to call the police. I'm numb! I am shut off. I don't feel anything. My mouth is closed shut with scared feelings to even breathe out loud.

I am horrified. Who is this person, and why is he doing this to me? I want to sleep, cuddle up in bed, run, walk away to be alone; not chatty.

I wish it would rain and wash away this sick feeling. I just need fresh air!

The Letters

Dearest F & S, (D's mother and sister)

I am photocopying this letter and sending you each a copy. So, while writing the letter to you yesterday, a counselor asked me to come to the office after dinner. FedEx came to drop off a direct letter to me. I was not aware of where it came from.

I reviewed the groupings of letters and photos that had been sent to me regarding D's resting place. To be direct, they contained words someone used to desecrate D, and, obviously, to hurt me.

I have been a wreck since then. The police were notified. They arrived here this morning to review the photos taken of the gravesite and read the messages. They issued a description of the threat/harassment with no clue as to who to charge at this time.

Today, while I was at self-esteem class, I got asked to the desk as another letter had arrived. It says derogatory words about me and the counselors who work here.

Included is a description of how they ruined the site where D was found. I'm upset to my stomach and completely have no idea how/why someone would do this. I felt I needed to tell you guys, and please make your Facebooks private. I'm going to ask my mom to do that with mine, so we don't get contacted by this sick person.

I really hope you guys are okay, and I'd love to hear an update or get a phone call when I'm out. Something to help heal our wounds. I feel for you and miss you both. I can't imagine what you feel, and I've been lucky to have this treatment center to help me cope with my grief.

I'm coming out of treatment soon, and I'm going to finish D's bucket list at some point. I can't do it alone, but I feel guilty if I let it go and his dreams die. Our relationship was and still is strong.

I'll keep in touch, just write me ASAP!

Love, Courtney

Dear F (D's Family, Letter #2)

I am writing to you from recovery. With the guilt and sadness of the 3 losses I experienced between February 22nd and March 8th, 2015, I realized I needed extra support. I've been clean from drugs for about eight years and drugs are the last thing I wanted to turn to.

My alcohol consumption was a concern to D over the years, as he was the one who went with me when I found out I have fatty liver. He always worried about me.

When I received his coin and AA book from you, I

went on a 3-day Bathtub Bender until my eyes were without tears. I had 16 bottles of wine in my system. That's when I got my roommate and my mom to bring me to the detox. I went to a women's facility, and now I am at a woman's trauma Mental Health Center.

During this time, I've been making life decisions, receiving support for my alcoholism, and working on my health. I've gone through so much.

D told me he had been working on his post-traumatic stress disorder since his overdose when he was 19 in Florida. He said he lost his long-term memories from age 15 and younger, and his memory started to clear during the time we visited him in that hotel he was staying at.

He opened up about one particular situation, back when he was living in the city, about his father who cheated on his mother. We took a motorcycle to Spring Ridge Farms to pick apples, fruit, etc. to make pies.

We used his laptop and watched movies, and this one time, in confidence, he opened up about why he hated his dad. He knew I would help, listen, and never judge.

I hope when I'm finished with rehab, we can talk soon.

Love you, Courtney

To Do List

Friday, May 1st, 2015

Recovery is a journey, not a destination. The walk keeps going because you don't want to fall off the face of the earth. We strive for progress, not perfection!

Things to work on when I get out:
1. Book writing (start on it)
2. Apply to school courses
3. AA meetings
4. Oasis meeting
5. Plan trip May 2-4 weekend
6. Plan pod party
7. Camping
8. Summer plans
9. Therapist appointment
10. Car
11. Life coaching
12. Health kick

I Have Changed

Visiting Day, Saturday, May 2nd, 2015

AR is coming today, and I need to breathe. I look forward to something good after a horrible couple of days. My heart warms when I see him. I feel home, reality, and love when he is around. Thank God today there is something to look forward to.

Page 19 in the *Living Sober* book is about changing old routines. This is the perfect thing to read at this moment. I guess they are right about our higher power showing us what to read. I didn't choose this book or information right now, but I need to hear this. <u>Do not do what I normally would!</u>

Change, remember, I am changing, and I have changed! I must show the world that I'm back to my normal, good self. The old me would run, drink, go crazy, and yell. Now, I don't do anything. Walk away; this is the right thing to do. Live and Let Live.

Walk away when these anger emotions or stubbornness comes through, just breathe, and walk away.

This too shall pass. I'm proud of myself at this moment; with control, less stress or anger, just facing the issue right away!

Alumni meeting
"I know whatever you ask for you will get, as long as you live, now it'll come."

That was DR with 7 years sobriety. She reminds me of my Uncle M. She is 65 and loves her cats.

She's talking about detox and how she could never imagine going one day without drinking, drugs, men, sex, pills, and overeating.

I'm having flashbacks from New Year's Eve, going with D to Pickle Barrel, and other situations like picking him up at the shelter, etc.

What was he thinking? When do I get the rest of his things? Where and when can I see him? Where is he when I need him?

Is he with me? Please, let me feel him here with me just sitting looking at the stars.

Smudging

Smudging Sunday; 35 days sober

I just got smudged. Take the smoking sage upon your face, head, ears, and your heart. They mentioned something about how AA works, and I just pictured myself asking my dad to come to an AA meeting, and I realize he'd be sitting there praising the fact of the invite but feeling uncomfortable. He would have his legs crossed, shifting, and shuffling in his chair.

I am living one day at a time here for me. Let others follow or let them go their own way. I need to keep reminding myself of this!

It's easier being a sober alcoholic than a drunk alcoholic.

4 pm meeting called How'd You Get Here?

I am partially numb to hearing people open up about how they plan their own deaths. I am also wondering why people would do drugs and drink to the extent that they plan to die.

Aren't they sad and concerned about all those they

will be leaving behind? I have wanted to hurt myself, to feel it, to get as deep and dark as I can get, but I'm sure I could never want to die.

Back when I was sitting in my washroom when I was younger, my boyfriend, M, and I would fight. I threatened to kill myself to hurt him. I'd listen to the same song over and over. I knew I'd cry and feel pain, slit my wrists, put Band-Aids on hoping it did not show but also that it would so I would get some attention.

In the past five years of being physically and mentally sick, I've been constantly yelling for others not to give me any attention. I didn't want them to see I was sick, physically or mentally. I want attention, but I don't want to break down. I don't want people to know I'm not as hard as I pretend to be. I want to be that intimidating person no one questions.

I'm uncomfortable even listening to others speak about near death experiences. They are so hurt. There are so many of us.

I am not alone, but if that's the case, are any of us unique? They say it's all about being unique. Do we really ever stand out?

Triangle = service, unity, recovery. It finally makes sense! Threesome!

Throw yourself into the program before you go back to work. Recovery needs to be your priority. Once you feel full, you'll be able to flourish and work at your career.

If you're depressed, you are living in the past, if you feel anxious you are living in the future. So, live in the now/today!

Sense of Connection

Monday, May 4th, 2015

I'm really thrilled about today. Every time someone uses the expression, "May the 4th be with you," I think about my friend's sister and how they'll be celebrating today, and I'm here.

Ash graduates today, which is a double-edged sword. My father's birthday and my nephew's birthday are today too.

Someone asked me if I'm writing a book, referring to my journal, if it is a self-published, personal experience monologue.

Number two on my to-do list is to create a book about my experiences in rehab. Even if 12 people read it and are moved in any way, I'll be pleased.

I'd love for those people to feel a sense of connection with me, and for the book to be a comfort when needed in a time of stress.

This disease is like my skin; it's there forever, and it will not go away. Recovery is possible for alcoholics who honestly want to stop drinking. It is a fatal disease.

Sometimes you don't need to deal with it; if you have to, it'll come through and you'll just know.

Live in the now and deal with it (addiction) when it comes, that's all you need to manage. When we're in relapse mode, we try to fill a void by going against rules and routines and by making excuses up.

This is one major reason why I go out of my way to do homework above and beyond, because if I just mindlessly fill it in, I'm already in relapse mode. I can do this; it's a lifelong decision. Do not give up!

One time, I yelled at J so much to just get booze, and I'm sorry I did so, he didn't deserve that. Whether he is mad or just going through his stuff, I need to apologize and create peace by saying sorry and meaning it.

I Can Only Live and Let Live.

Sorry, no matter what!

There is no mystery about it, addiction to alcohol is a poisoning within our body. The recovery is to recognize our alcoholism and admit our physical illness.

It makes us humble and willing to stop.

Real alcoholics are sick from poisoning acquired by substituting alcohol for food and rest.

Physical health can be restored, but no cure will permit us to become controlled drinkers.

Fatty Liver

May 5, 2015

I have come to realize today (reaffirmed) that I do not enjoy this current version of learning.

This takes me back to my school years and finding there are book-smart people and there are street-smart people out there. I want the discussion to be around, "What does this mean to me? What do I think they're saying? What do I feel?" which are all open to interpretation. The exercises we are doing are just word-for-word. I don't feel like I'm intrigued or learning, but rather being force-fed baby food, and I don't enjoy it.

This is one of those times I learn to unlearn and be comfortable in this uncomfortable situation.

My bones hurt today. I am in low pain but crampy in my joints and body. I am looking forward to relaxing and wondering how we are to cope with pain without drugs or alcohol.

I just realized it's Mother's Day coming up. I'd like for my mom and sister to have a special gift from me!

I can work on cards as an activity.

Today, I should be having my review, I have one week left until I graduate!

My definition of a higher power is: Someone like my mom, greater than myself, an inspiration, a unique role model, takes care of me when I'm sick, tucked me into bed safely every night, and hugs me when I'm down. A smile that is so bright, it colors my world with beautiful color. You're not perfect, mom, but you're my rock! I love you for me. If coincidences persist, it's an angel trying to tell you something!

I miss you again today, D. I'm doing so well. You were with me so much of the last year, and I don't remember most of it. :{

Turn your drinking room into your recovery room. AR and I should frame photos, paint, and make a meditation room with a map of the world and find a payphone to put in it.

How important is writing to me? It's everything!

Some of the girls and I got 24-hour desire chips for one of the girls who needs us tonight. I got my one-month chip tonight!

Those days sitting at the shelter being devastated, going on the road with D's mom and sister, the funeral, tattoo, etc. I really should go back over it all and write it out.

This evening, the older group of women are just hanging out playing Euchre. I feel like I'm in an old film watching them sit around playing cards for quarters. I can imagine them with a smoke in hand, drink beside them, and hearing the jokes flow. Reminds me of my grandma.

Dr. T. came in today to review any concerns with our blood work, and the pee test lady came in as well. After drinking three not-needed sodas leading to an overly full bladder, I walked into the waiting line on the third-floor hallway only to see a dog there.

I asked the doctor if she could tell me my liver score.

I know it sounds stupid, but I just remembered yesterday that I have a liver disease! Oh, I guess it just doesn't disappear.

My fatty liver disease is about 3 years old now. I last got tested after D took me in to see a doctor because we had gone on a bike ride in the winter, and I bruised my legs.

He was so concerned about how I bruised like no one else and that they didn't go away. He took me to my doctor's appointment and was with me when I got the sad result. I had Fatty Liver.

We went to the bar after, and I said I wouldn't drink anymore and cut back. He said he tried too. Average liver scores are 28 to 40. Sadly, I got called in the same day for results of 1195.

I did start on healing for a bit until my Celiac came around and made me panic. I got involved in fixing that and forgot about my liver.

Like a new toy for a toddler, when they told me

my liver score had dropped to 675, I screamed with joy. She looked a bit concerned, but because she knew of my disease and prior number, she was extremely ecstatic for me.

Other girls question their scores of 56, maybe 70 the highest, and I laughed with joy!

How is it I'm still alive?

Higher power, D, whomever, thank you for this. I can only imagine my results next week when I leave here to get the comparison. I am so thrilled. Doctor C should see me now.

Addicted to Recovery

May 6th, 2015

My grief is turned up high today.

I asked for a one-on-one. Debe is here today, and I like her. I'm wondering why this is happening. Mel mentions that our higher power will give us things when we're ready.

Is this D trying to come through and tell me something? I know I won't get the why's answered.

The time you feel like a drink or using, that should be when you're working on recovery work. Work, work, work. There is no timeline, it doesn't happen quickly, it just happens, and you'll know.

My family has been patient with my decision to go to rehab. I must be patient with them regarding their support, help, and trust.

I haven't thought about or felt I needed or wanted a chill pill.

I have had this "walk away" tattoo for my coping and as a warning until I came to rehab, and now I see it having a different, more positive meaning.

I don't want others to struggle, but I take too many sicklings in and worry I'll forget to take care of myself.

We reviewed our first meeting, and I was able to go back in my book and see exactly how I felt. I've come a long way from when I first entered detox.

I'm addicted to recovery, but I do kick some down time to not think about this every minute of every day. Some TV or a movie!

Day 40 Sober

May 9th, 2015

Day 40 sober! My sister is coming today. I'm excited to see her and my niece.

We're talking about mindfulness, saying it's being a hundred percent in the moment. We use some substance to avoid observing in a mindfulness way.

I completely forgot all from Halloween through February, lost in my mind, and then pieces, then sobriety. Detox is still a shock!

I love both of my sisters and shared about it today at the meeting, then burst into tears. I feel better now.

To Dos

Monday, May 11th, 2015

Bring your family to an open meeting (family program for explanation) to help them understand what we are.

I wonder how we decide on a fellowship or support because I can become an addict again anytime. I need to not do too much too soon when I leave, and be careful who I hang out with.

I'm just a step away from a new beginning, coming from addiction and leaving a better person and successfully sober.

I find a smile and compassion for others. I am not the same person who came here; I am similar in body but a new person. I am not afraid of my old weakness and alcohol.

My Goals:

Commitment to AA

God, clean house, help others

Your intellect is back and meant to be used

90 meetings in 90 days
Bathe in sobriety and then routine
If it works today, why not try it tomorrow?
Places and things not to slip
You drank with those who drank like you to fit in.
Now, you hang out with similar people who don't drink
No, thank you; they aren't concerned
Only people fearful of sobriety knock it
Be on guard in unguarded moments
Rediscovery of self

Recovery

Tuesday, May 12th, 2015

 I completed my program. I'm happy and sad at the same time but excited to get started on my new life!

I know I haven't written much lately, but I've been busy: meetings, meetings, and more meetings. I feel incredible! I am so proud of myself, and I know D is proud of me too.

If anyone reads this, I hope they will find peace and hope in whatever trauma they are going through!

Recovery is a journey, not a destination. You did it! One step at a time.

PART TWO
PATRICIA'S JOURNAL
A Mother's Journey

"You were the light that is blinding me,
You're the anchor that I tie to my brain,
'Cause when it feels when I'm lost at sea,
You're the song that I sing again and again.
All the time, all the time,
I think of you all the time."

The Anchor by Bastille

May 12, 2019

I knew when I had such a great Mother's Day that the feeling could not last!

I heard from all the kids that day, Beau and Lea, my stepchildren, and Courtney, my daughter.

Courtney, her boyfriend, Rich, and I went out for Mother's Day brunch. I was surprised she made it. She brought me a card and a present; a small cow stuffy because she and her girlfriends call me "Mom-Moo." After they left, I was on my own because Christie, my husband, was away in Germany for work. I took a quiet moment to relish the feeling of happiness.

I took the time because I knew in my gut something bad was going to happen. I could tell Courtney was extremely sick when she was here; sicker than I had ever seen her. Despite the long blonde hair that sported her signature bow, the false eyelashes she wore constantly, the freckled face and bright green eyes, I knew something was wrong.

Rich said she had been throwing up blood, had a fever, and spent Saturday in bed all day. He said he suspected she had slipped up and had a drink. Knowing this, I was surprised she pushed herself to make sure she could spend Mother's Day with me.

Her alcohol abuse and damage to her liver was not a revelation. We had been battling this problem for over five years with many attempts at rehab, therapy, tough love...you name it, to get it through her head that she was on a path to self-destruction.

At 28-years-old, she thought she was too young for her liver problems to be anything more than "bad liver scores" on her blood tests.

But deep down we both knew, we all knew, she had pushed her limits way too far. During her last bout in the hospital, at the end of November 2018, the doctor told us it was bad. He said she could never drink again, or she would die. He scared us, and she began an intensive out-patient program for addiction. Since the beginning of the year, she continually claimed she was sober.

Prior to Courtney's hospitalization in 2018, I had spent a week in the hospital for a flare up of COPD and chronic bronchitis. I have been fighting COPD for years, but that fall I was extremely sick. When they told me I would be in the hospital for at least a week, I looked at the doctor and said, "If I am going to be here that long, then I am sure I will go through detox!"

You see, I had a drinking problem too. I never felt like I was an "alcoholic," just someone with a nasty drinking habit. I mean, I never lost my job or license, and it hadn't affected my life. At least, so I thought. I believed I was like any of my friends; I drank at lunch and would continue until bedtime. EVERY DAY!

My drink of choice was vodka. Whenever we would visit friends and they would ask, 'What can I get you to drink?" My husband would reply, "Patricia drinks vodka and anything!" (It is so easy to mix vodka with every-thing, that is why I loved it.)

I detoxed in the hospital, and right after I was re-leased, Courtney was admitted for the first time. When I saw how ill she was and given I hadn't had a drop of alcohol in over seven days (without dying, just mentally going nuts for a drink), I realized I could never touch vodka or any other type of liquor again!

How could I be a hypocrite and tell my daughter she had to really quit drinking this time while I go right back to the bottle? As I am writing this, I am five days away from six months alcohol-free! No one I know would EVER think I could give up drinking.

I knew the best way to help my daughter was to be a role model. If I could do it, so could she! Courtney con-tinually told me how proud of me she was and always claimed she was sober too.

After the hospital, and as we entered 2019, both Christie and I had suspicions she was having "slip-ups." We could tell by the way she acted if she was sober or drunk, even though she would deny the latter.

Her boyfriend Rich, confirmed our worst fears when he told us he repeatedly found gin hidden in camouflaged containers, like water bottles, around the apartment. Courtney would become defensive and deny any of his accusations. It was causing some friction in their rela-tionship. No one likes to be lied to. We were grateful he kept us informed of the indiscretions he suspected.

My mother's intuition told me something was wrong two Fridays before Mother's Day. Courtney had asked if she could borrow money to give Rich for rent. She said her job had "changed their pay schedule," and she would pay us back the next Friday of Mother's Day Weekend.

When I spoke to her the next Friday and asked if she had gotten paid, I got a long line of bullshit that criss-crossed from a problem with the direct deposit she had just set up to her saying they had mailed it and she didn't receive it. The story made little sense, but we were used to that with Courtney.

I couldn't contact her all day the Saturday before Mother's Day, and we talk every day. When I finally reached Rich early in the evening, he told me she was in bed all day and had been throwing up blood.

Even though I said it was okay to postpone Mother's Day, they came anyway. The first thing I noticed when they arrived was how yellow the whites of Courtney's eyes were. It was horrifying to look at. She was thin, jaundiced, bruised, and her psoriasis had returned. We went out to eat, but I could tell it was a struggle for her to get through the day.

She took a selfie of us, and the picture made it clear she was not well. I tabled any discussion about where her paycheck was and didn't confront her about drinking. I just focused on her getting to a doctor ASAP on Monday. She said she would call work and her doctor and let me know the plan in the morning.

We then spent a quiet afternoon watching TV after brunch. We sat next to each other on the couch and held hands. I kept looking at her, and a sick feeling developed in my stomach.

When I kissed her goodbye, I had a sinking feeling that this might be the last Mother's Day we would ever spend together. I didn't want to think that, and I tried to get it out of my head, but I could not shake the eerie feeling that something bad was going to happen.

May 13, 2019

I woke up on Monday feeling excited. My great friend from Canada, Christy H., was coming to visit me for the week. (Not to confuse this Christy with my husband, Christie, who Courtney affectionately called Big Daddy, so I will refer to him by that moniker, LOL). I hadn't seen her in three years, since I moved from Toronto to Arizona. This was her first visit to the state, and I had a week full of activities scheduled for us. The timing was perfect because Big Daddy was away, and I was thankful for the company. I planned to make her visit a real girls' trip!

I received a text from Courtney saying she had an appointment with her doctor at 9:30. Feeling optimistic: a new day, a friend coming, Courtney going to the doc. I headed to the airport. Waiting for my friend in the cell phone lot, Courtney texted that they were sending her to Banner Health ER for blood work, fluids, and monitoring.

After picking up my friend, we headed to Cave Creek to show her the house and get settled. On the way, I got another text from Court:

"Waiting for an IV and vitamin pack. Hope you

don't worry too much until you have to!"

"Oh boy," I replied.

She texted again...

"So far as I know...they are keeping me. Going to run tests and may do surgery. Waiting to hear more."

What? I was shocked by the word surgery but knew how Courtney could exaggerate. I texted back, "I'll try calling after lunch." Truthfully, I wasn't that worried as she had been in and out of the hospital so many times. Christy asked if we should go right there, and I said, "She's in the right place, and there is not much we could do today, anyway. Let's get you settled and let her get settled, and we will go see her tomorrow."

I felt a little guilty, but I have spent years jumping through hoops for Courtney. Today was my day.

Courtney was good with that, saying, "Rich said he would come after work, and I have my frog, Bertel, in case they poke me with any needles," she laughed. She always had a HUGE fear of needles, so I was proud of her for being brave and understanding that I had out-of-town company.

May 14, 2009

My phone dinged with a text that woke me up. Of course, it was Courtney,

"In case you're here, and they end up choosing to do the surgery while you're here, they have a huge bistro and shopping area!"

What is this surgery she keeps talking about, I thought as I answered her, dismissing her warning as probably not being as urgent as she was making it out to be.

"LOL, just going to walk Grayson (our Maltese Yorkie), and we will be on our way."

"The first part is about an hour, and they are doing the bigger procedure at 1 pm."

"Okay, we will try and get there as soon as we can. Still not sure what she is talking about.

"Oh, I need eyelash glue, LOL."

Well, it can't be that bad if she is thinking about her fake eyelashes!

What she was calling surgery was an endoscopy to see why she had been throwing up blood the day before Mother's Day.

I felt anxious as we arrived at the hospital but was

happy my friend, Christy, was with me. When I turned into the valet parking lane, I ran over a median and thought I scraped the car.

"I am such a terrible driver." We both just laughed.

We headed to Courtney's room, and when we entered, she was gone. A lady was standing there. Fear and horror ran through my veins when she introduced herself as the chaplain.

"Oh my God, is she okay?" I asked nervously.

"Oh, I am so sorry to scare you, we are just here to help comfort the family. Your daughter was just taken for some tests."

"OMG, you scared me!"

"Would you like to speak with me? Perhaps I can provide some healing words during this time."

"I'm not sure what you mean by 'this time.' My daughter was brought in yesterday, and she just texted me this morning."

"Perhaps this isn't a good time," the Chaplain said softly.

"Yes, please, I don't mean to be rude, but I haven't even seen my daughter since she was admitted. It really scared me to come in and find you here and her gone." I was starting to feel like I was in a movie or something, but she got my message and left.

"What an introduction to Arizona this is for you," I chuckled with Christy. "First the car, then the Chaplain, what is next?"

Well, the doctor was next. Courtney arrived back in the room, and the doctor wanted to speak to both of us. Christy politely excused herself and went outside.

The doctor explained that the veins in Courtney's

esophagus were enlarged due to serious liver disease, and that is why she had been throwing up blood.

"Courtney, when did you have your last drink?" the doctor asked.

"May 10th, I slipped up and had a drink," Courtney said, averting my eyes and looking right at him. That was the Friday before Mother's Day!

A wave of shock, anger, and confusion shot through my body. Courtney had been attending an outpatient therapy program and talking about going back to school to become a rehab counselor. She wanted to give back. We had started collecting purses; she had an idea! There was so much she wanted to do. Why in the world would she drink? What was she thinking?

"Your daughter's liver is over 80% damaged; she has stage 4 cirrhosis of the liver. She can NEVER drink alcohol again!" he informed us rather abruptly.

"What does all this mean? Can't the liver repair itself?" I questioned.

"Not when it is this far damaged. The only cure at this point is a liver transplant. She is a candidate for it, but you have to be sober for six months before they will put you on the list."

"Even if she might die without a new liver before we get to six months?" I was horrified.

"That's the rule. Do you understand, Courtney? You cannot touch alcohol at all, even a sip of mouthwash with alcohol will adversely affect you."

Courtney nodded and looked stunned.

I thanked the doctor, and he said the endoscopy would be at 1 pm. I sat for a moment and didn't know whether to cry, yell at Courtney for drinking, or try to compartmentalize my feelings because I had to be strong.

The rest of the day was a blur of tests, waiting, and trying to keep our spirits up. I told Christy I would take her to dinner, kissed Court, and told her to text me later. I was happy Rich, her boyfriend, could handle the "night shift" so I didn't feel so guilty.

I took Christy out for a nice dinner. I was almost six months sober and kept thinking, if Courtney hadn't slipped up, she would be able to go on a transplant list right away since we both quit at the same time.

During dinner, I missed having a glass of wine and would have loved to wind down with a beverage, but I kept thinking of her condition and stayed strong.

My dinner came, and I realized I was hungry. "Bon Appetit," I said to Christy, took my first bite, and broke a tooth.

May 15, 2019

I woke up at 4 am angry! Mad that Courtney had slipped up, mad that I was sick again, mad I lost a tooth, mad my husband wasn't home, just mad!

Feeling frustrated, I decided to write the following email to my friend, my sister, and my sister-in-law to update people on Courtney's condition.

Email sent...

Courtney went into the hospital on Monday because of her liver. On the first day, she was given a blood transfusion. I was able to meet with her GI doctor at the hospital on Tuesday morning.

Courtney has cirrhosis of the liver. 80% of her liver is damaged beyond repair. She is currently operating with only 20% of her liver. Due to her failing liver, she also has esophageal varices.

Esophageal varices are abnormal, enlarged veins in the tube that connects the throat and stomach (esophagus). This condition occurs most often in people with serious liver diseases.

The vessels can leak blood, or even rupture, causing life-threatening bleeding. She was throwing up blood this last weekend. So, on Tuesday, they did an endoscopy and had to 'band' 4 enlarged veins. As you can imagine, her throat is very sore, and she was on a clear liquid diet until yesterday when they started to introduce soft foods. She will have to have the procedure repeated in 4 weeks.

After she gets out, probably Friday, she will be seeing her GI specialist every two weeks. They are referring her to the Mayo Clinic where we will begin the prep for what ultimately will result in a liver transplant.

She needs to stay completely free of alcohol for 6 months before they will put her on the list. As far as how long the wait is for a liver, or length of recovery, we don't know until we go to the Mayo Clinic.

If Courtney drinks any alcohol, she will die. Both doctors (the GI and Endoscopy) gave us a serious talk saying she could become a statistic and not see her 30th birthday unless she adheres strictly to the rules.

As you can imagine, listening to both doctors, we have been in a state of shock. It felt surreal listening to the doctors giving us the warnings. They both said they were sorry they had to be so blunt, but they wanted to make sure Courtney and I understood the severity of her illness.

I know it's a lot of information, and I am sure you will have questions now and over the upcoming months. I can give you more details when we talk.

In the meantime, I've had my friend visiting me this week so have had to juggle that with having bronchitis again (went to urgent care yesterday). I also cracked a bridge on the left side of my mouth and have not had time to call the dentist. Last night, a tooth fell out on the right side. Unbelievable! I am calling the dentist today!

I'm sorry to break the news by email, but there

hasn't been a good time to call. I am sad and scared but trying to take it a day at a time. Courtney feels the same, but she sounds much better after having had some food. This is going to be a long process.

I love you all so much.

May 16, 2019

Today I had planned a party with some of my friends so they could meet Christy. I spoke with Courtney in the morning, and she sounded better.

"Have fun at the party, check in when you can," she reassured me. I felt I needed a day to take a break. However, I was nervous because I planned to tell my friends at the party about her condition but wanted to wait till after lunch.

Everyone was supportive and asked if there was anything they could do. I reiterated that she was in the best place and, hopefully, will get out on Friday but just wanted everyone to know.

I received really nice emails from my sister and friends I had reached out to yesterday.

"Patricia, so, so sorry to hear this. If there is anything I can do, please don't hesitate to ask. I guess the good news is she is under medical care. Hopefully, this is the turning point for her."

"It sounds like they made it real. Other than guiding her through the medical maze, that is really all you can do. The rest is up to her."

"I feel so bad for you with the bronchitis and dental

problems. But you need to take care of yourself too. Ugh, I feel your pain for it all. I will call you tonight to check in and let you get your day going. I am sure you have a lot on your mind. Remember, I AM HERE!"

"Please call anytime. Bermuda is just a trip; you are family, and I am here for you. Love you, hugs, and hoping for all the best for you and Courtney. Hugs, Kat" (My sister)

"Dear Patricia,

I don't know what to say. I wish I had the courage to call Courtney and give her some sound, heartfelt advice. It just isn't right. I am so sorry for what you are going through, and Christy, what a trip for her, thank God she is there to be a support for you. She is your friend and loves you both, so I am sure she is more than understanding and supportive.

"Again, I wish I was closer. Times like this make me sick to my stomach and miss you so much.

"I wish I could hug you both and tell you it is going to be okay. It will work out, it always does. Courtney is strong, and she will survive this too. NO MORE ALCOHOL should be the easiest part of all of this.

"Sending love and hugs from here." Nadia (My best friend)

"Omg...I know you said Courtney had mentioned a liver transplant once before but did not know how severe she was. I don't know if I could have remembered everything that they told you, as you did. My heart just goes out to you...

"The doctors were very blunt but maybe this will help Courtney to not drink, if she was. Do you think she was sneaking some drinks? Can they tell if she has been drinking? Omg, omg...

"Try to enjoy today, stay strong, and prayers and good thoughts for both of you.

"See you soon. xxoo

"Be high-spirited every day!" Carol (My very good friend)

May 17, 2019

Woke up again at 4 am; guess it's my new wake up time. Christy has an early flight. I plan to take her to the airport then go to the hospital and wait for Courtney to be released.

Today is going to be a busy day because after I get Courtney settled, Big Daddy is arriving from Germany, and I am picking him up. Two airport runs today!

"Good morning." I received a text from Courtney at 7 am.

"Morning! So happy you are getting out today. Getting ready to go to the airport; will call as soon as I can."

"NP, I'm just waiting on breakfast. My blood pressure is 94/53, hopefully, they won't bitch about it. They already did blood work and meds."

"I've got a cooler full of food to bring to your house."

"Great, thanks! I'm making a grocery list for you; I need a few specific things."

"I'll see you soon, love you."

"Love you, Mom."

They were bringing Courtney down in a wheelchair, so I thought I would park outside and wait. Little did I know I would be sitting there for 2½ hours in the Arizona heat!

My heart just went out to my little girl when I saw them roll her out, clutching her frog and looking VERY weak and thin. She barely had the strength to get into the car.

We arrived at her apartment, a second-floor walkup. She had a hard time making her way up the stairs and immediately laid on the couch.

I was horrified when I placed the food I brought over, onto the kitchen counter and saw what I saw. This is so disgusting and embarrassing, but her kitchen was infested with bugs. When I turned on the light, they scattered in every direction.

"Eeek!" I screamed at the top of my lungs, "Courtney, these bugs are out of control, you have to call the manager!"

"I know, I know," she replied from the couch, "I've been bitching about it to the landlord for weeks, but they haven't done anything."

"I think I'm going to be sick; this totally creeps me out!"

"Mmhmm, that's what I've been saying, and no one listens to me."

I was pissed. How could she stand this? I didn't understand why she hadn't taken or demanded action.

"It's because my name is not on the lease, so Rich has to talk to the management company," she tried to explain.

I was livid and psychotically driven to kill these bugs. I pulled out all the food, plates, pots, and pans, only to find hordes of bugs scattering about. It was a major infestation.

"You just can't leave any food out," she called from the couch while I frantically tried catching and killing the bugs. I was creeped out, exhausted, and had extraordinarily little patience left.

"I'm going to Fry's (supermarket) to get you some food, pick up your prescriptions, and buy some bug spray and traps. I'll be back soon." I stormed toward the door. How the hell can this kid live in these conditions?

"I'm just going to watch TV and rest on the couch," she called.

"Ok, see you soon," I replied, a bit sarcastically. My mind raced all the way to Fry's. I felt bad because she was sick. How are we ever going to get to the point where she would make it to the transplant list? Why did she have that drink? I feel bad, but really, she has done this to herself.

It took me four trips up and down the stairs to bring everything up to her apartment. I was sweating, it was hot, and guess what? The air conditioning wasn't working. I wanted to just scream.

I proceeded to disinfect the kitchen, spray, set up traps, and put away all the food. I gave her the meds she needed to take and created a list of med times and doses for Rich.

Then, I took her dog, Bryer, out and checked on Courtney before I left. Her stomach was swollen, she was dozing on the couch, and she looked frail.

I felt guilty for being mad at her. I kissed her forehead and said, "I love you." Then I said a silent prayer to help us both find the strength to get through this.

I left to pick up Big Daddy at the airport.

May 21, 2019

I spent Saturday and Sunday with my husband, thankful Rich was able to do the "weekend shift." I needed the down time and tried to bring Christie up to speed on Courtney's condition. Early Monday morning, my phone dinged.

Text from Courtney 6:15 am:

"Morning, Lady, let me know your thoughts. Was thinking I could meet you at the dentist, we could grab something to eat if you're up to it, get gas, and come back and watch a movie. Love you."

"Morning to you. I had a horrible sleep. My dentist is out this way in Union Hills. When I get to your place, we can get gas and try lunch. Problem is, I probably can't eat after dental work, and you hardly eat anything. Also, I just spent $350 on groceries for you! We will get gas and see. Maybe manicures instead of food? Please take your pills this am. How was your night?"

"I slept through the night, woke up only once. Rich had to get up early to go to the VA for blood work. I'm down for manicures, then we could do lunch here, for sure. Thought it was your dentist in Phoenix. Why did you have a bad sleep? I'm just having some tea and watching a comedy show in bed. Staring at a bug, LOL."

"LOL, I hate those bugs! I woke up every flipping hour! I had a major earworm song stuck in my head. I couldn't get it to stop, ugh! My dentist has an office out here; we switched offices when we moved."

"Oh, that makes more sense. I hate earworms; I'll even get one line stuck too and can't stop it until I listen to the song like five times in a row. I'm just making an egg and toast and going to take my meds."

"Good girl!! I know it was two lines, and it's still going round and round in my head! LOL, I'll text after the dentist when I'm on my way. Love you."

"Sounds good. Good Luck."

"Big D made us chicken soup. It's delicious. I'll be bringing that with me!"

The dentist informed me it would cost $3,800 for an implant and $3,400 for a bridge. I wasn't looking forward to telling Big Daddy about the bill.

Christie arrived back from Germany and was pretty jet lagged. I told him, in detail, about Courtney's week in the hospital, Christy's visit, and my missing tooth. We spent the weekend helping him get settled. I warned him that Courtney was sick. Understandably, he felt anger at first because she had put herself in this position. I asked him to be gentle when he saw her.

In the meantime, I went to Courtney's apartment after the dentist and was greeted by the ongoing bug-a-palooza! It seems none of my traps or spray helped at all.

"Let's get out of here and go get our nails done!" I exclaimed, not able to stand another second in this 'roach motel.'

We went to a nail place, and I could tell Courtney

was weak. She was also jaundiced, and her stomach was so bloated she looked nine months pregnant. She was finished before me, so she went to sit in the pedicure chair. She turned on the massager and immediately fell asleep.

I felt terrible, like maybe I shouldn't have taken her out, but I could tell she was restless being home. I took her back afterwards, and we had lunch and planned for the week ahead: follow up with doctors' visits, oil change for her car, and schedule a time for them to tap her stomach. Hopefully, getting rid of the fluid will make her feel more comfortable.

I received an email from my work friend, Eric. I am close with him and his wife, Suzanne. For some reason, Courtney has always loved Eric Barber. He sent the following email. I read it to her:

"Hey Patricia,

"Suzanne has filled me in on events in Phoenix. I am not often at a loss for words as you are aware, so allow me to do my best.

"Please convey my love to Courtney and tell her that when she becomes my third wife, I will need her to be healthy.

"In any case, I will pray for everyone there (Yes, I am a bit weird these days), and if there is anything I can do, let me know.

"With all my love, Eric"

Courtney smiled her beautiful big smile, then she teared up. "Mom, I'm really afraid," she whispered.

May 22, 2019

Text from Courtney 6:01 am:

"Morning, Lady! What time are you going to be here? We need to get something for my tummy. It's so swollen still. It hurts :("

"Morning! Will leave here at 7. So sorry you're miserable. I slept better last night, so I'm ready for the day. Love you."

"My stomach is like 4 times the size, and it's hurting my back badly."

"Leaving now."

It is exhausting driving back and forth, but I make it in time for the follow up visit with the primary doctor at 9:20 am.

Turns out, her primary doctor is a nurse practitioner. She prescribed lidocaine patches for her back, wrote the referral for the chest X-ray, and a referral to the GI (who we were able to schedule with for the same day). She also checked her vitals. Her weight was up by 16 pounds, all from fluid in her stomach, and her BP was 77/43.

Then we headed to the chest x-ray, let her sleep for half an hour, got patches at CVS, and woke her up for the 30-minute drive to the GI doctor's office.

He laid out a plan, a very somber and long plan; a six-month plan to get her on the list. He said if she does not get a transplant, she probably won't make it to her 30th birthday.

I contacted Banner to schedule an abdominal tap appointment for tomorrow.

Courtney is not doing well. Her skin and eyes are bright yellow, and she has pneumonia. Went to get blood work done, only to find it's by appointment only. Both of us were frustrated and cranky when we got in the car, and it didn't help that I drove over a huge screw in the parking lot and got a flat tire. We drove to Court' s with my hazards on.

Called Big Daddy about the tire, grabbed Courtney's car, and headed off to get her prescription, only to find out she needs to go in and get it herself because it's a narcotic. Headed back, picked her up, got the meds. Whew.

Rich or Big D will have to fix my car. Blood work will have to wait until tomorrow. I need a break, and Rich was on his way home.

I text her after the crazy day:

"Home! I'm totally exhausted. There are two new episodes of the Amazing Race tonight."

"What time does it start? Rich says he LOVES the soup Big D made."

"So glad he likes it. What a day, eh? LOL, we are a pair. It was like we were on the Amazing Race today." I smiled, picturing us on the show.

"If the Amazing Race had a detour consisting of "run over curbs and screws and get as many doctor visits done in one day :)"

"Bahahaha, add flat tires to the roadblock! Hope you sleep okay. Love you."

"Love you more, Mom! Thanks for your help."

May 23, 2019

Hello Family and Friends!

I want to thank you all for the kind words, love, and prayers you've been sending. It means a lot to Courtney, Christie, and me! I am sorry I have not had time to personally reach out, but it has been a busy week of doctors and home care.

Courtney was released from the hospital last Friday. In addition to the diagnosis of stage 4 cirrhosis of the liver, she also had acute blood loss from the variceal bleed, low hemoglobin, and pneumonia.

As you can imagine, she is very weak but gaining a bit of strength each day. Her blood pressure is extremely low, averaging 77/44. Her skin and eyeballs are severely jaundiced.

She has an accumulation of fluid in the abdominal cavity which is called ascites. Ascites is common in people with cirrhosis, and it usually develops when the liver begins to fail. She has gained 16 pounds of fluid since her release. They are scheduling an abdominal tap, or paracentesis, a procedure to remove excess fluid from the abdominal cavity, for 1 pm today.

This week, we had the follow up with her primary

and the GI doctor, who laid out a plan and told us what to expect over the next few months. We had a follow up chest X-ray, blood work, and scheduled the repeat endoscopy for mid-June.

We plan to bring her to our house for the long weekend. Perhaps those of you who are local may want to come visit her. I think she would like that.

In the meantime, I made it to the dentist, and I need an implant or bridge for the tooth I lost, roughly $3,800! Yikes! I saw my primary, and she is treating me for pneumonia. I am on my second round of antibiotics and steroids and have an appointment with my pulmonologist today.

When Courtney and I were out yesterday, I ran over a screw, drove precariously back to her place, and now I have a flat tire!

On the upside, it has been delightful to have my personal chef, Big Daddy, home to cook me dinner each night.

If you are on this email, you hold a special place in our hearts! I hope everyone has a wonderful long weekend (or had one, my Canadian family).

Love you all so much,
Patricia

After writing this early morning email update, I took Courtney in to get her first tap done. The plan was for me to take her, have Big Daddy meet us there, then I would go to the dentist, and he would take Courtney back to her apartment.

I stayed in the waiting room when they took her for the tap. She texted me pictures of the first load of fluid they drained, and I was thinking how much better she will feel getting rid of all the liquid she is carrying.

Big Daddy arrived, and like a relay, I updated him (Courtney was still in the back) and headed out to get my teeth worked on.

I finished with the dentist and figured everything was on track when I got a call while driving home. It was a nurse from the office where the tap had taken place.

"Courtney needs to go right to the emergency room. We just got her blood work back, and her hemoglobin is so low we suspect she is bleeding internally."

Confused, I ask, "Isn't she still there?"

"No, we let her go home before her blood work was read."

"Okay," I said hyperventilating. "I'll have to call my husband. I am forty minutes away from where she lives in Tempe."

I called Big D, and he was more than halfway home. He turned around and went back to get her.

I sent her a text, "Hey, did the doctor get ahold of you? Your blood levels are way off, and they need you to go back to the hospital. Big D is on his way and will bring you in. I'm sure you're upset about having to go back to the hospital!"

She texted back, "Here goes my fucking life. Fuck, all I've done to be good. I'm about to cry. Going to pack a bag."

"I'm soooooo sorry," I replied, glassy-eyed.

"Why didn't they just keep me then? Why didn't they check my blood work before releasing me? Fuckers! Are you coming to the hospital?"

"On my way."

Apparently, Big Daddy had to pound on the door because she was sleeping. Needless to say, Courtney was pissed. She grabbed Bertel, texted Rich, and Big D took her to the ER.

When I made it to the hospital, she was still waiting for a room but had an IV and other tubes hooked up to her.

Thank God for Rich. He showed up and said he would wait with her. He is an awesome guy and loves her so much. Big Daddy stayed with Rich and Courtney until she got a room. I was thoroughly worn out, worried, and nervous about what was to come. I went home and tried to sleep, but just after midnight, I was woken up by a text from Courtney.

May 24, 2019

12:14 am text from Courtney:

"I have my own room, which is really big. They may ask me if I want to go on life support if needed which makes me very, very scared, and depressed. I feel like every time I move one step ahead, I fall 10 steps backwards. :(I just want to be better. I love you so much, you are my world. Please come early tomorrow. I need to give them all the details of my medications so they can give them to me. I can't name them, so they can't give them to me without proof. Try to get some sleep, Mom."

2:50 am text from me to Courtney:

"Hope my text doesn't wake you. I'm up in the middle of the night, so worried. You are being brave through all of this, and we will conquer this. My heart aches you are going through this. You are my life, you are my sunshine, you are my Austria. I'll come as early as I can. I love you."

6:12 am text from Courtney:

"I'm in the worst pain of my life...I need you."

This was the last text I ever received from Courtney.

I went to the hospital at 7:15 am. Court had texted she needed me, was in the worst pain, and they were asking about life support. Multiple organ failures today: liver, kidney, GI, etc.; doctors swarming.

She is in the ICU. Hemoglobin down to 2, catheter in, not peeing, kidneys failing, internal bleeding. Did ultrasound, blood transfusion, need to do CT scan to determine area that is bleeding. Need her to lie still, sedate her, and put a tube down her throat to breathe for her. Had to give consent for procedure, stent put up the artery through the groin, sprayed or tied the bleed off, hoping it won't rupture, think it was from the abdominal tap the day before.

Belly swollen, extended, too weak to do a tap; hooked kidneys up to dialysis hoping that will kick start them back working. Drs said the next 24/48 hours would determine if she could live.

Told us to call family and tell anyone who wanted to talk to her. Called and texted everyone. Left at 6, Rich going back at 8, plan to get there early tomorrow.

Afraid her body is just shutting down; it is heartbreaking and horrible. We are all praying.

Please God don't let her die. My heart couldn't bear it.

I am at the hospital; they are trying not to put her on dialysis or a feeding tube, and I am waiting on the plan for today from the doctor.

Courtney is in horrible pain, and because her liver and kidneys are failing, they are limited as to what pain meds they can give her.

She is in too much pain to talk. How did this happen so fast? We were together yesterday and laughing about the tire. I don't understand.

They say it is really serious. I am scared and afraid.

May 25, 2019

At the hospital early at 6:30 am. She is the same as last night, waiting on the doctor for the daily plan. Hemoglobin is still low, getting more blood. Will be on dialysis for days.

Today's focus is measuring her hemoglobin because when they give her a transfusion, it goes up, but when they check her four hours later, it has dropped. Afraid there is still internal bleeding. By 4 pm, hemoglobin is holding, so that is good news.

Her belly is swollen, and the surgeon says she has Abdominal Compartment Syndrome. They will measure the fluid to see if it is causing compression of her vital arteries, nerves, or organs. They will have to give her medication to temporarily paralyze her to see if the compression is reduced. Not enough, so they will have to do a tap.

The only concern is that it could create another bleed like the first one she had, hoping it won't. If she does have an internal bleed, they will have to go back in and cauterize it. We are hoping they won't need to. If she gets some relief and hemoglobin stays up, the nutritionist will give her some liquid nutrition through the tube.

Estimated time the feeding tube will stay in, a few days to a week.

Dialysis indefinitely. It is heartbreaking seeing all these tubes and machines hooked up to my little girl. This feels like being in a bad movie; how can this be real?

May 26, 2019

Called in at 5:30 am to the overnight nurse. Some good news, she pooped 3 times last night, hemoglobin was at 8.2 and dropped slightly to 7.8. The nurse was going to check with doctor about more blood. Said she had a good night.

Yesterday, our neighbors Phil and Linda, texted that their pastors would come to the hospital and pray for Courtney. At first, I wasn't sure but felt some spirituality would be good and, at least, there was a partial connection to the pastors.

For some reason, I pictured the pastors arriving in ceremonious red robes, but I couldn't have been more wrong. Pastor Mike was a tall, white, Chicago guy, wearing jeans and a t-shirt (he also has a 28-year-old daughter). He was accompanied by Pastor Jimmy, Indian, short, and dressed fashionably. The church is Southern Baptist. They made the prayer ceremony very personalized; we all held hands and held Courtney's hand as well.

It was very special and comforting.

After praying, the doctor came in, the hemoglobin was dropping again. They shipped her off to CT to find the source of bleeding, then will work on stopping it. It's not a big bleed but still a bleed. Big D told me to go home, and he would wait with Rich.

I picked up Grayson, spoke with Lea, and told her about the pastors. Been almost 2 hours waiting to hear. She didn't get back to the room till 7:30 pm, and they couldn't find anything after three hours of searching. The poor kid must be exhausted. Big D got home at 9 pm.

Both of us are sad and frustrated that they can't find the source of her internal bleed.

May 27, 2019

Dear Pastor Jimmy and Pastor Mike,

Thank you for taking the time to come visit us at the hospital yesterday. You are both amazing and compassionate individuals, and I can see why God chose you to spread his message.

You made us feel comfortable by not making the day about a specific religion but about life, spirituality, and our darling daughter, Courtney.

The prayer session was comforting and hopeful.

After you left, they spent 3 hours in an exploratory session trying to identify the internal bleeding that won't stop. We are hoping to see some glimmer of progress today. She will remain sedated today and on dialysis.

Please continue to keep us in your prayers. God bless you!

Sincere thanks and love,

Patricia

"Good morning, Patricia!

Thank you for your kind words of encouragement. We will continue to pray for Courtney. Be strong and courageous. I want to leave you with this one passage from God's Word that has always encouraged my heart. Expecting great things from God!

Don't worry about anything, but in all your prayers ask God for what you need, always asking him with a thankful heart.

And God's peace, which is far beyond human understanding, will keep your hearts and minds safe in union with Christ Jesus (Philippians 4:6-7).

Sincerely, Pastor Jimmy"

May 28, 2019

Hello Dr. LeStourgeon,

My daughter has taken a turn for the worse. She is in ICU, intubated, kidneys have shut down, on dialysis, and liver is barely working. The doctors said yesterday they do not believe she will make it past 30 days. As I mentioned, she is only 28. They have told me to tell family and friends now is the time to come if they want to see her.

I am heartbroken, sad, and scared. I wanted to ask for either Clonazepam or Xanax, just enough to help me through until I can get back in to see you. If you need to see me, I will make an appointment but am spending all my time at the hospital right now.

I'm sorry to ask for this by email, but I can't sleep; I'm heartbroken, and the last thing I want to do is start drinking again. I appreciate anything you can do for me during this nightmare. Either way, I will set up a follow up appt., and if need be, squeeze in sooner regarding a prescription.

Thank you, Patricia

Is it only Tuesday?

Last Tuesday, we did the follow up appointment. at her primary and the GI on Wednesday. How the fuck did everything go downhill so fast? I still don't understand.

Ventilator turned down, breathing on her own all night and all day so far (4 pm). She opened her eyes a few times, rolled them and closed them again, but a bright spot in the storm. They haven't tapped her belly again, hopefully they won't.

May 29, 2019

Having a moment of Zen.

At the hospital alone and waiting for the first wave of people to arrive tonight. Courtney had a stable night, and she opens her eyes more and more, good thing. Bad thing, she is in pain, confusion, and stress.

It's absolutely heartbreaking.

They keep giving her small, steady amounts of pain-killers to take the edge off, but because she is awake, they need her to hang in through this phase so they can maybe remove the tube tomorrow. The other reason they can't give too many pain meds is because medications are processed by the liver.

Kidney doctor came by again today, a different one from yesterday. Basically, they keep confirming her kidneys have completely failed, still a chance of revival but very slim.

None of my clothes are fitting, and the next wave of people are coming tonight. Need something that is comfortable for the hospital, but not sloppy; warm inside, lightweight outside, not falling off my butt.

Bought a pink tracksuit. So cute and comfy, and it felt nice to do something for me. Sent my sister selfies lol, sent my girlfriends a text. Of course, Carol has now offered to go shopping for me. Her forte, you know? Of course, she will take that on.

When people ask what they can do, it's interesting that you have a hard time knowing what to ask for. But Linda and Phil provided the pastors, Noah sent me music to play for Courtney, Carol, my friend, brought comfortable clothes for me to wear in the hospital, and my sister is sending short encouraging videos for me to play for Courtney. It's as if they all knew exactly what we needed.

May 30, 2019

Can't Sleep

3:30 am. Can't sleep, but the clonazepam helped me get a good, solid five hours.

Nadia brought some of her dad's meat from Canada! She said you should have seen them at the border questioning. Bahaha. I had the idea of hanging them from the IV tower like they were in the cold room and taking a picture.

I spent the day alone with Courtney. The good news is she breathed a whole day without the respirator, and we hoped today would be the day they'd pull it out. They also reduced the sedative and pain meds. The goal was to get her conscious enough to respond to commands, nod yes or no, wiggle toes, etc.

She was very restless, and you could tell she was in pain. Her facial expressions were heartbreaking. She kept flipping her hands and feet around.

I had to ask Nadia if she thought I was exaggerating, or if she really was in a life-or-death situation. Nadia confirmed, it was critical and so tragically sad. She said she was shocked when she first saw her.

Family is starting to arrive today, and more are

coming tomorrow. Having everyone around is comforting but frightening. It confirms how seriously ill Courtney is, and the future does not look good.

May 31, 2019

"Dearest friends and family,

For those of you who do not know me, I am Nadia, aka Aunt Nod to Courtney. This note comes on behalf of Patricia, Mike (Courtney's dad), and Christie, in order to update you and provide you with some important details if you are planning to visit. As of last evening, the latest update is that Courtney's blood pressure is stable, her breathing is good, although she remains on the breathing tube (which is down her throat) because without it, there is not enough oxygen going to her brain, so the tube must remain connected to assist her and keep her alive. Also, she is on dialysis as her kidneys have stopped functioning, and this is working to support her.

She continues to have internal bleeding. They have repaired tears twice, and each time is very critical, again, her arteries are thinning, and blood flow is a concern. Her hemoglobin is unsteady, it continues to fluctuate, and every time they repair an internal bleed or add to her blood supply, it poses a serious threat; anything slight at this point could tip her over. Her liver, the ultimate concern, remains nonfunctional, which makes her jaundiced and leaves her in the unfortunate state of being gravely ill.

She has not had any food for over 7 days. They have tried feeding her through a tube through her nose, which leads to fluid just sitting in her stomach. They had to drain that along with the toxins building up, all of which makes her belly bloat. She must be less than 100 lbs. at this point, so she doesn't look much like herself; other than when she opens her eyes and you see those brilliant green eyes, her beautifully freckled face, and imagine her precious smile.

Folks, I tried to best paint a picture for you all, to see what we see, living moment by moment in recent days and in the days to come.

The current update from the medical team is that Courtney remains very sick, any little thing could tip her over: a small bleed in an artery (as the tube stays in), continued lack of nutrition, and being poked in most parts of her body with tubes of some kind. They did begin with some vitamins (liquid) and some other liquid nutrient to supplement the glucose (she is connected to 8 various drips), but she could leave us at any time and begin her after life journey.

Unfortunately, this seems more and more like the reality. We are praying and know there are prayers from everyone for Courtney to get through this and recover to a happy, healthy Courtney. The truth is, we are not sure she can last long enough to take that long road to recovery. We have not been given a time as to how long she can stay like this; the medical team cannot say, her status can change literally within an hour.

It is best for anyone who would like to visit, to do so, sooner rather than later. I will provide alternative accommodation options below if there is no more room at Patricia and Christie's home in Cave Creek.

Also, I ask that you respect their wishes to continue praying. Thank you on their behalf for your love and support. Also, please limit your outreach, it is such a difficult time, and updating everyone at different times is so straining, repeating these details is unfair to ask of them. Until I was here, I wanted to know as well, "How is today? Are there any changes? Just let me know when you have a minute..." I have been here 1.5 days and have slept a total of 7 hours combined. Patricia, even less.

To show your love and care during this time, respect their wishes, and know that someone will reach out as soon as there is time to decompress and breathe.

Based on what I heard from the medical team, if you would like to visit Courtney, you should come sooner rather than later. If you wish to visit after Courtney's hospital stay, this as well would be welcomed, and there will be another communication to follow.

Patricia, Christie, and Michael (Courtney's biological father from Toronto) are so blessed to have the love and support from you all. Since the situation is so grave, Patricia, Christie, and Michael want to spend as much time with Courtney as they can. Understanding and respecting their time is so dearly appreciated.

Everyone on this list will be updated when there is something different to tell. If there is no communication, then there is no update. We are not given any false hopes by the medical team and best sharing messages as we receive them. We may not be given notice, or much more than 1 hour, if Courtney tips over, so, again, be aware of this, and use this information to help make your decision of whether to visit.

With love, Aunt Nod"

June 2, 2019

Fuck you, liver!

This day went to shit. Yellow drapes, infection, gloves, two meetings in the conference room.

Power of attorney, DNR, and keeping her comfortable. Her boyfriend, Rich, in tears. We went home at 7 pm. Nadia made wings. Back at 10 pm, moving forward with providing comfort.

She may die tonight, or tomorrow. We don't want to let her go, but she is suffering.

It's not fair.

It sucks, she's so young, she only slipped up once, why is this happening???

Fuck you, liver!

June 4, 2019

We received a call at 3 am and were told to come back to the hospital to say our goodbyes.

Big Daddy, Mike, our son Beau, and I headed to the hospital to say goodbye to Courtney.

How can you say good-bye to your darling little girl, your princess, your 'twin,' your best friend?

I am so sorry this is happening and feel guilty, like I should have done more.

We were there in time to say goodbye and tell her she was loved.

"Goodbye, Courtney," but it doesn't yet seem real. It is an empty expression.

June 5, 2019

Email from Nadia

"It is with unbearable sadness that we announce the peaceful passing of Courtney Elizabeth Michaels, 28 years old, on Tuesday, June 4, 2019. She died from kidney and liver failure at the Banner University Medical Hospital in Phoenix, Arizona.

Courtney is predeceased by her best friend and loving mother Patricia, stepfather Christie, her father Michael, stepmother Rachel, siblings Beau (41), Lea (39), and Lauren (19), dearest nephews, Derich (8) and Oscar (5), and her precious niece, Sophia (5). She will also be missed by her countless loving friends, family members, and fur babies in both Canada and the US.

A Celebration of Life will be scheduled for mid-July in Toronto, Ontario. Further information is forthcoming. Heartfelt gratitude to the wonderful doctors and nurses who took care of Courtney over the last eleven days. The family will announce a charity for donations to be made in Courtney's memory at the celebration this summer.

With love, Nadia"

June 6, 2019

I'm in a black hole. I am surrounded by people who love and care about me, but I feel empty. This cannot be true. Courtney can't be gone. We were texting, we went and got manicures, we laughed at my poor driving, they had let her out, she had gone home, how the hell did this happen?

My emotions are attacking me with a vengeance. Horror, heartbreak, guilt, denial, and intense sadness. I am in shock. I am grateful to have family and friends around, but feel a sense of hopelessness, even though I know they are trying to comfort me.

I am doubting God. How can there be a higher power and be so cruel as to take my daughter from me? I'm angry at God (if He is there) because this is a cruel joke. That's what it must be: a joke. Someone will tell me it's not true.

I'm exhausted but can't sleep. I don't want to eat or shower. I have anxiety, I'm restless, I don't know what to do. I feel like I don't want to live. I feel like I can't face what's ahead of me.

I can't bear to not have Courtney in my life.

June 8, 2019

I am that person!

I'm 'that person.' The person I never wanted to be, but here I am. You know, the one everyone whispers about when they enter a room? The one they look at and say, "Isn't that the woman whose daughter died?" Yes, I am that person. My daughter died at 28, and the sad part is an addiction ended her life. Now, I am that person.

If you recently had a loved one die, then you are that person too. What becomes awkward is suddenly people don't know what to say to you, and you are the one to help them feel more comfortable. You say, "Thank you for your words, don't feel bad." "Don't be sorry, it's not your fault," and "You're right, I am sure they are in a better place."

Then, when the obligatory exchange of "the right thing to say" happens, people turn the conversation to more light-hearted topics or to talking about themselves...and you're left being that person. You nod and respond to the chatter that barely registers with your brain while internally screaming *Can't you see I'm grieving?*

Grief is an emotion we don't like to talk about,

maybe because it's an emotion we don't fully understand. Grief can happen to anyone suffering a loss of any
kind. It doesn't have to be a death. It could be the loss of
a relationship, a pet, or a job.

Grief happens when someone or something you love
disappears from your life. For being one of the most
powerful and debilitating emotions, it's the one we feel
most uncomfortable discussing.

Joy, happiness, anger, sadness, and love are emotions we can speak about for hours. We usually give poor
grief a few cliché sayings and never allow it to be the
core of a conversation. It's not anyone's fault, it's the
way we have been raised and what society deems appro-
priate.

"Give it time," "I know how you feel," and "You
have to keep living" are the very statements you don't
want to hear.

You don't want to give it time, that denotes you will
somehow "get over your loss." You never get over it.

And no, you don't know how I feel. You may have
had a similar experience, but your bond with the person
who passed is unique to you and that person. People may
understand that you are grieving, that they have experienced comparable emotions, but every individual's grief
is unique.

Yes, we must keep living, I agree, but it doesn't
make the grief go away. It becomes an accessory to our
daily life, like an ankle bracelet; not overly noticeable
but part of you with every step you take.

The griever is also in an awkward position. If we are
too happy, others might think we didn't care about our
loved one as much as we proclaim. If we walk around

sad and sound like Eeyore, we feel guilty for bringing everyone around us down.

There is no right answer for how to act or feel around others. Triggers happen without any notice, and the smallest most inconsequential thing can ambush us with a surge of grief. I tell everyone, "My grief comes in waves, so I try to breathe when the tide is out."

For those suffering a recent loss or continuing to mourn the loss of a loved one, I say embrace your grief. You will never be whole, you will never be fully healed, but remember, grief equals love. If you did not love that person, you wouldn't be grieving. The deeper the love, the more intense the grief.

Take your time, talk to those who will listen, shed those tears, and hold your head up high. Become 'That Person'—the one who is not afraid to grieve and show it—not just 'that person' everyone is whispering about.

PART THREE
PURSE-IMPRESSIONS

"To gift rehab graduates with a purse or backpack that celebrates their accomplishments, allowing them to move forward with dignity, strength, and the knowledge that someone cares."

June 12, 2019

Email to my girlfriends,

Hi Girls,

Thanks everyone for your support during this terrible time.

You might have heard me discuss an idea Courtney had of giving back to the rehab centers she had gone to, especially the one she was at in Canada. She thought every girl should have a purse to carry her stuff out in when graduating rehab. It wasn't dignified to leave with just a plastic grocery bag, especially after doing something positive for yourself. This way, the girls could make a good "Purse-Impression" when they officially enter recovery.

So, I have an idea. I would like Courtney's memorial to be impactful as it was important to her to help other addicts. As sad and hard as it is for me to say it, what killed Courtney was her struggle to beat addiction.

What I am proposing is that people donate purses in lieu of flowers. We can also ask for items to stuff the purses with or money to buy the items ourselves.

I have spoken to Celina, Courtney's oldest friend, and she is willing to spearhead the event for me, since I am in AZ and the service will be held in Canada. The plan is to have this happen at her memorial on July 13th. We can bring the stuffed purses to the church and donate them after the service. I have picked 7/13 for the memorial because those were her favorite numbers. We are not sure why, but she had them tattooed on her wrist.

I am excited about this idea, and it helps relieve the pain knowing I can turn something negative into something good. What do you all think?

If anyone has any ideas or ways they would like to contribute, that would be wonderful, however, this is not a solicitation email. I'm just sharing with my friends how I am managing my grief. I still can't believe she is gone.

Love,

Patricia

June 13, 2019

Today I got the most awesome email from Celina. It looks like we are going to make Courtney's dream come true.

"Hi Patricia!

I've done a bit of digging, and this is what I've come up with today.

I spoke to the manager of the women's house at Renascent Munro Treatment Centre. I told her about Courtney's idea and asked if it could be of benefit to the other women there. She was over the moon excited!

She **loved** the idea of something for the women LEAVING treatment, something they would receive at graduation to take with them out into the world :) She said it was a beautiful idea.

She actually took out her own purse and started going through it, and together we came up with a list of items for a woman to carry with her to make a good "purse impression."

She also stated how powerful it would be to these girls if there was a small business card or postcard in each purse with a little message from Courtney. She said the girls who will receive Courtney's gifts are the lucky ones, the ones getting another chance and the opportunity to make it as a sober person out in the world. Knowing Courtney's story may help them succeed!

My question is about how people can donate. I'm thinking we keep it as simple as possible. Maybe we can make up a flyer or social media post and share it with people.

People can then:

1) Donate a purse before the memorial. I can set up a drop box at my work.

2) Bring a filled purse or bag to Courtney's memorial on July 13th.

3) Donate money to the cause if they can't make it to the memorial in person. We can set up a website, such as GoFundMe, and use the money to purchase items to fill the purses. Then we can bring the filled purses to the memorial on their behalf.

I think this is off to a good start! My friend has already talked to a few drugstores that are willing to donate items, so I will send her the list and get started! Let me know what you want to do about the flyer/post so we can get the word out. One month exactly!

LOVE YOU

xo

Celina"

June 14, 2019

God bless Celina, Courtney's long-time friend who is like another daughter to me. Celina's mom, Judy, and I have been friends since the girls were toddlers.

Celina's enthusiasm and "get it done attitude" have energized me. I have a focus; I have a purpose, and I feel it is important for me to do this.

I don't know what will happen with Purse-Impressions after the memorial, but even if we just do this one event, we will be making a difference in people's lives.

I am not sure how many purses we will get, or how or where we will fill them, but we are going to do it!

Things are happening quickly. I set up a GoFundMe page, and my friends helped me create a website and a Facebook page.

I miss Courtney so much it aches, but I know she would be thrilled to see her idea coming to life.

June 18, 2019

Everyone is so excited about this idea! I think this is therapeutic for all of us because we can't believe Courtney really is gone. I think we might get a lot of purses. It seems like the word is spreading fast.

Just reading the description on the GoFundMe page makes me think this might turn into a great charity. I think addicts are forgotten, and everyone knows someone affected by addiction. Maybe this could be a good thing for me to do in my life right now.

I've heard registering a nonprofit is not easy; best to get a lawyer. Maybe I should explore what it takes when we get back to Arizona after the service.

GoFundMe
Contribute to Courtney's Tribute
Make a Donation!
Courtney Elizabeth Michaels
January 7, 1991- June 4, 2019

Patricia Brusha lost her darling daughter last week to addiction. Courtney Elizabeth Michaels, 28-years-old, passed away suddenly and unexpectedly in Phoenix,

Arizona on June 4, 2019, due to cirrhosis of the liver and kidney failure.

Courtney spent time in numerous rehab centers in Toronto and Phoenix. Thankful for the help she received, she always gave back to them as much as she was able to. One of the things she felt strongly about was being able to leave rehab feeling strong and with dignity.

When someone arrives at rehab, it's not under the best of circumstances. When they leave, it is usually with their personal items in a plastic bag. Courtney and Patricia spoke about providing each rehab graduate with a purse they could call their own.

In Courtney's memory, Patricia is leading the initiative "Purse-Impressions." She is collecting purses and essential items for the Renascent Center Toronto, Ontario to give to women reentering the world after rehab; if only to let them know they have value and are not alone.

Courtney was passionate about trying to help others while working to free herself of addictions. Although her organs failed in the end, it was her addiction that took her life.

We will combine our celebration of life memorial for Courtney on 7/13 with our first "Purse-Impressions" fundraiser. We do this in Courtney's name to help put an end to addiction.

July 11, 2019

We had an insane purse packing party!! I am blown away by the generosity and enthusiasm everyone has displayed on behalf of this charity donation. It's unbelievable!

According to the stats:

- Over 300 purses were collected (more will arrive at the memorial)
- 246 are stuffed and ready to go
- 60 unstuffed to be donated
- 18 men's duffel backpack-type bags
- Shopper's Drug Mart donated two bins full of items along with

- 9 - $10 gift cards.
- 21 clock radios
- ·Raised $2,000 to buy items for the purses and backpacks

We will have a sample on display at the event, but the majority will be ready to be loaded up for whoever comes to get them. I don't even know how to begin to thank everyone who just jumped right in. Thank you, God. I love you, Courtney!

July 13, 2019

The Memorial, The Eulogy 7/13

"Welcome, everyone to Courtney's Celebration of Life and our inaugural fundraiser for Purse-Impressions. I sincerely want to thank all of you for taking the time to come celebrate with us today. A special thank you to those of you who have traveled from out of town to be here.

"My darling little girl, Courtney! I cannot believe she was taken away from us after only 28 years on this earth. It was way too soon, but the moments and memories we had are precious and will live within us forever.

"Courtney brought joy into our lives from the moment she was born.

"Courtney was only 5 when Christie came into our lives. I don't know exactly how it started, but she always called him Big Daddy and embraced him as a father figure her entire life. It thrilled her to inherit two siblings, Beau and Lea, when Christie and I got married. She adored having a big brother and sister and always bragged about them and about being the youngest!

"Well, that was until Lauren came along, the daughter of Mike (Courtney's dad) and his new wife, Rachel, who, like my friend, Judy, was a tremendous help in helping me co-parent during her school years. At that point, Courtney became an older sister, the youngest child, and an only child!

"She loved the diversity in her family and her nationality, owning dual citizenship in Canada and the USA since birth. She had wonderful experiences with all her aunts and uncles, and she cherished the moments with every one of them. Courtney was bigger than life! She lived large. Go Big or Go Home; 100% on everything she did. She was bursting with energy, passion, and a gusto for life. Courtney maintained her childlike enthusiasm and sense of wonderment until the day she passed.

"She loved to laugh. She loved to have fun. She sincerely cared about the people in her life. She had a habit of reaching out spontaneously to let someone know she was thinking about them, cared about how they were doing, or just wanted to tell them she loved them.

"Quirky people and their stories fascinated Courtney. She possessed a magical ability to have people open up to her, just minutes after meeting them. She could easily repeat their whole life story. She was able to do this because she asked questions, she listened to answers; she remembered details and lived vicariously through other people's life adventures. It was one of her many redeeming qualities.

"Courtney loved telling stories as much as she enjoyed hearing them. In fact, she was a master storyteller. She could weave a tale using truth, exaggeration, and imagination leaving the listener scratching their head and saying, 'Is that true?' With her claiming, 'I swear it is,

I'll send you a picture!'

"Courtney's childhood consisted of traveling on weekends to see Big Daddy and Beau at the house in Warren, Michigan. One weekend a month, she would help me as manager on duty at the Dodge Suite Hotels, learning the hotel business from a young age. It was there she met her lifelong, self-appointed aunt, and my best friend, Nadia, her Italian Zia.

"Courtney loved to laugh, take selfies, wear sunnies, scrapbook, and chat with friends. I made her watch all my favorite movies and musicals. Over and over, we watched *The Sound of Music, Grease, Hair, Across the Universe, My Best Friend's Wedding, National Lampoon's Xmas Vacation*, and more.

"She had a special place in her heart for her friends, especially Kelsey, Sam, and Celina.

"She loved all genres of music and couldn't accomplish anything without a soundtrack running in the background. She loved dogs, cats, kids, and most of all, frogs! She believed in miracles and unicorns.

"In her way, Courtney was very spiritual, believing in signs (7/13) and knowing things happen for a reason.

"She was an old soul for such a young woman. With those sparkling eyes, she never saw what the rest of us saw. She looked in her own distorted mirror, never seeing the incredible beauty the rest of us saw in her.

"Never, ever did I think God would decide to call her home so soon. There were many long, agonizing battles the last few years, and she fought like a warrior every step of the way. Addiction, however, won the war.

"The outpouring of love and support our family has received is beyond overwhelming. When I wrote Courtney's obituary, it was my intention to tell the truth, hoping it could help even one person beat their addiction.

"Before she left us, Courtney and I discussed an idea of how to give back, because, at that point, she thought she had won the battle.

"She didn't like that when women graduated from rehab, they often left there with their personal items in a plastic bag. She wanted better for them; she wanted those women to hold their heads high, to be proud of their amazing accomplishment, and to leave with something that showed their value. That was the birth of Purse-Impressions.

"Little did I know how it would take off. Many friends, and friends of friends, have donated purses and money. In Courtney's memory, we will honor, congratulate, and celebrate over 400 women taking their first steps into the real world with their addiction behind them and their lives in front of them. Purse-Impressions has become my life's calling, allowing me to perpetually honor the life of my daughter while hopefully sparing other mothers and fathers the sorrow I have had to experience.

"My beautiful Courtney…I hope as you look down from heaven you are FINALLY able to see how much you were adored, admired, and so, so loved.

"The number of people who have been affected by your death is a testament to the impact you had on everyone you met in your 28 short years of life.

"Courtney, you are, and always will be, a special person. Your kind and generous spirit lives on and continues to shine brightly. You are an inspiration. As your mother, I could not be prouder. Keep working those miracles from heaven. I love you to the moon and back, forever and always."

September 12, 2019

I made it through the summer even though I felt hollow and empty. We went to see the grandkids in Wisconsin and Michigan after the memorial. I was struggling. After the memorial, I mentally crashed, and grief hit me like a tsunami! I was lonely, withdrawn, and missed Courtney more than anyone could imagine.

There had been so many people around when she passed, then there were all the people at the memorial, and now it felt like coming down after a high. Reality set in quickly, and I was second guessing and doubting myself about the charity. Would this really work?

True to my word, I hired a lawyer, and today I received the corporate book and the letter from the IRS. It's official! Purse-Impressions is now a registered 501 (C) 3 nonprofit corporation.

My sister, Kathy, and my friend, Carol, became my board members, and we held our first board meeting. Top of the list: find rehab facilities interested in participating in our program. Sounds easy, doesn't it?

Both Kathy and Carol started looking in their neighborhoods, Palm Beach and Denver, while I started to tackle AZ.

I approached the two facilities that Courtney had gone to, the place where I did my intensive outpatient program (IOP), and cold-called the local rehab in Cave Creek. The responses I got ranged from, "Sure, go ahead and make a donation," to "We have to talk to the board, and they will have to vote on it."

They didn't get it. They didn't understand this was an idea Courtney had and that each purse was a symbol of hope and encouragement. I was discouraged, and Kathy and Carol were having a hard time finding places too. I just wanted to crawl into bed, curl up in a ball, and hug Courtney's frog, Bertel. Then, out of the blue, I received this email from Canada:

"I graduated from Renascent just over two weeks ago. I have a few purses I would like to donate for purse-impressions. I also wanted to say thank you! I was the first person to receive a purse, and I think what you're doing is amazing, and I genuinely appreciate it."

This email warmed my heart and gave me hope! I was bound and determined to find a place that would understand the mission and its potential impact.

Courtney, darling, I'm not giving up. I believe in your idea, and by the grace of God, this will happen!

September 22, 2019

My sister found a rehab in Florida, a small sober living house, and they were excited. Purses and money continued to come in, and I was determined to find just the right place to participate in the program we were creating. Today, I had a bright spot. I received a report from Renascent that touched my heart and made me even more resolved in my mission.

Report From Renascent (sent to their distribution list):

The Vision

A group of family, friends, and loved ones gathered on Saturday, July 13th to celebrate the life of Courtney M., a Munro alumnus who passed away suddenly and unexpectedly on June 4, 2019 due to cirrhosis of the liver and kidney failure.

Courtney spent time in rehab centers in Toronto and Phoenix, Arizona. Courtney always wanted to give back. She felt strongly about people being able to leave a treatment facility with dignity, feeling strong and ready for the next chapter of their lives.

In Courtney's memory, her mother, Patricia B., and

friend, Celina, have partnered to lead an initiative called "Purse-Impressions." The aim is to collect purses and essential items for Renascent to give to women who are graduating and heading back out into the world having completed their inpatient treatment stay.

They collected nearly 600 purses filled with self-care items in just a few short weeks.

The Project

It is not uncommon for those entering or leaving a Renascent treatment center to arrive with their belongings in a plastic bag or spilling out of their arms because they often come to us from an unstable or temporary living situation. It was Courtney's wish to provide graduates of Munro, and other treatment facilities, with a purse they could call their own. The goal is to let clients know they are not alone, they have value, and they are people.

The Process

Our Munro Treatment Centre houses 25 to 28 clients each month from across the province. Munro is a unique, home-like environment that provides a safe, person-centered approach to addiction recovery. From the first steps into Munro, you know you are going to create memories, build healthy relationships with women, and be in an open space to share and feel safe.

Clients often stay for a duration of 28-35 days, depending on their program.

Upon completion, thanks to the generosity of Courtney's friends, family, and loved ones, our clients have been able to walk away from Renascent with a little extra pep in their step.

To date, Munro staff has provided 16 women with gently used purses filled with toiletries, essentials, and various items to help them feel good about themselves as they embark on their recovery journey.

Clients "shop" for their purse and select one that fits their style, personality, and funky spirit. All clients who received purses were grateful for your generosity. They all enjoyed reading the special card you prepared for them.

Some clients have said:

"I can't believe this is for me!"

"Wow! There are so many to choose from."

"This one's perfect for when I go to my first interview."

"I have no words, thank you so much."

"Thank you!"

"I will treasure it always."

Thank you, Patricia, and Purse-Impressions, for making such a memorable, impactful impression on the powerful women who seek services from our Munro Centre.

October 1, 2019

Finally, a breakthrough! I spoke with my grief counselor and explained that I was having a hard time finding a rehab to participate in the program we had developed.

She pulled out her phone and said, "Let me Google facilities near me and see what I find. Well, I'll be damned; there is one on the first floor of this building." She put her phone down and declared, "Let's go see them!"

It turned out to be a very fancy, expensive outpatient facility, but I explained about our charity to the girls at the desk, just in case.

"I don't think your program would be a good fit here," one of the girls explained, "but my boyfriend works at Crossroads, Inc., and I'm sure they would love the idea!"

Tears formed in my eyes, and although I left feeling defeated, my therapist helped me look up Crossroads, and, suddenly, an idea popped into my head.

"What if I make up some sample purses and bring them with me on a cold call?" I asked my therapist, "Even if they don't like the idea, I can donate the purses I bring."

Energized, yet again, I went home and packed up a dozen beautiful designer handbags and planned to drive to one of their facilities the next day.

Terrified, I pulled into the entrance only to see a sign in front of me stating, "All visitors must check in with the office."

There were numerous people hanging outside the front door smoking and talking, probably clients of the rehab. They all stared at me as I nervously walked past them clutching my box of purses.

Inside, there was a flurry of activity, and I wasn't sure where to go. A random girl asked if she could help me. I inquired if there was a manager available that I could speak to.

"I can go get someone for you," she replied. "Can I tell them what it's about?"

"I'd like to make a donation," I responded, hands shaking and heart pounding.

I waited an eternity before a young girl, not much older than Courtney, approached.

"Hi, I'm Ashley," she greeted me brightly, "What can I help you with?"

"I have a donation," I started to explain with tears welling up in my eyes. "But, there's a special meaning behind it, and I was wondering if you had a few minutes for me to tell you about it."

"Sure thing," she chirped, and I felt relieved she was willing to listen to me. "Let's go into my office, it's too crazy out here!" She laughed. I followed her to a small room with a desk pushed against the wall and a solo chair. She asked me to wait a minute as she ran to get me a chair from another room.

She introduced herself properly and told me she was a former patient at the facility. She proudly declared she was a recovering alcoholic and had recently become manager of this location.

Choking back tears, I told her my story of how I had lost my daughter, Courtney, her idea of helping women graduating from treatment, and about the purses I had brought with me today. To my surprise, she was absolutely thrilled and delighted!

"This is the best idea I've ever heard!" she enthused. "Would you be able to supply purses as their Christmas presents first?" She continued, speaking rapidly, "See, there are a lot of girls currently in treatment. They don't get anything for Christmas, and we're starting to think about that now. In fact, the district manager, Donna, is here today and was just talking about Christmas at our morning meeting. Let me go get her so she can meet you."

Anxiously, I waited for what seemed like forever. When Donna walked into the room, I immediately felt as if Courtney had sent me an angel.

She gave me a fabulous hug and said, "This is absolutely unbelievable! We were just talking about doing a purse drive for Christmas at our morning meeting, and you show up out of the blue! I'm sure this was meant to be! Now, my dear, tell me all about Courtney!"

I burst into tears; I was totally blown away! It seemed like a miracle. It *was* meant to be! Surely, a gift from God and Courtney.

Donna loved the idea of the graduation program and was excited we could help for Christmas, as well. Suddenly, I had a lot of work to do because I needed to get ready for our first Arizona delivery. This was happening! Courtney's dream was finally going to come true.

God bless you, Donna!

October 2, 2019

Subject: RE: So wonderful to meet you!

"Hi Donna,
I can't tell you how much it meant to me to meet you yesterday and receive one of your awesome hugs! I believe we both happened to be there at the same time for a reason. I immediately sensed your energy and passion and our shared connection for inspiring these young ladies to "stay strong."

For Christmas, we are going to donate 45-50 stuffed backpacks to the women's house. Additionally, we will be donating 100 purses for the graduation program. I think it was a great idea to use backpacks for Xmas and save the purses for graduation. We would like to deliver the backpacks on Monday, December 16th. I am blessed to have found Crossroads and the special people involved in the organization. I look forward to hearing from you soon.
Patricia B."

January 20, 2020

"Dear Patricia,

Thank you, Patricia! It was such a beautiful day on Christmas and a touching experience to be together and share in the Purse Impressions legacy. I am so proud to be a part of this.

The girls look so cute with their backpacks, and they were wearing them every day to group. Thank you again for these!! They absolutely LOVED them.

It moves me to see how Courtney continues to find ways to show you she is with you. That warms my heart. Thank you again for all you are doing for our clients. It is such an amazing blessing.

Here is the picture we took; we can't show their faces, but they all had smiles.

Love you!!
Donna"

192 Courtney M.

193 Purse-Impressions

Mother's Day 2020

I just realized that I haven't written much since meeting Donna last fall. Ever since that day, everything has exploded, and the charity has gone from 0 to 60 in a flash!

We were busy in December stuffing backpacks for Christmas and purses for graduation. All the stuffing was done out of my house. My poor little place looked like an Amazon warehouse!

Both my sister, Kathy, and Carol found places to make Christmas donations as well, so by the end of 2019, the charity was up and running at full speed.

We held our first fundraiser on February 23, 2020. The event was called "Bags and Brunch," and it was a tremendous success. We had a silent auction, entertainment, and a wonderful luncheon.

Everyone had a great time, and Donna and Beth, the ladies from Crossroads, both attended. They brought a donation check with them and a significant donation of purses. I was stunned by what I was seeing. I also could not believe how full my house was going to be when I brought the big box of purses home!

We added two more rehabs to our program bringing the total up to five, two in Arizona, and one each in Florida, Colorado, and Canada.

We made money at the fundraiser, had a decent supply of inventory, and the charity, by all counts, was turning into a huge success!

Then, in early March of 2020, right after the function, Covid hit. Everything shut down, the world shut down, and we were in lockdown.

I kept wondering about my girls and guys in rehab during this time. We had donated purses and backpacks for their graduations, but we weren't able to visit anyone.

As I came down from the adrenaline high of the fundraiser and plunged into this new world of Covid, I started to get depressed.

Then today rolled around, Mother's Day, one year after I started writing. Courtney's anniversary was approaching quickly. I was sad, and I wrote a note to God.

Are You Busy, God?

Are you busy, God? Cause I have a few questions if you have the time.

Like, why did you have to take my beautiful, charismatic daughter, Courtney, so early? Why did you allow her addiction to alcohol to be stronger than her will to live? Why didn't she listen to the doctor or the rest of us?

I know she tried and tried and struggled and struggled. I could tell she was very sad inside. She knew she had a problem. She would have given anything to get better but could never get the monkey off her back completely.

I don't think she knew she would die. I know she knew she was very sick. It scared her. She had slipped up. Why did this slip up put her over the edge? Were you too busy, God, to see how she was drowning? Or is this the way you saved her?

Are you busy, God, because I need answers? The pain I feel is physically debilitating. I can't believe it's true. I cannot believe I will never talk with her again. Never hear her laugh. Never hear her call me mom. Now, no one calls me mom.

God, do you see her? Have you met her? If you have, you will not forget her! She is memorable with her large personality, infectious laugh, and great beauty inside and out.

Are you busy, God? If you could take a moment and please tell her I miss her. That I am heartbroken, but I am not mad at her. Please tell her I love her and always have. That I feel I should have done more, but I believe she knew how hard I tried to help her beat her addiction.

God, I know you're busy, there is so much tragedy that happens every day. It must be hard to take care of everyone, especially now with Covid. But please know how much I would appreciate it if you took a moment and let my little girl know that she is special. That everyone loves her and misses her. That she made a difference in so many lives. That her mom loves her to the moon and back. Forever!

Thank you in advance. If you are not too busy, God.

June 15, 2020

I made it through the 1-year anniversary day! I am so proud I did it.

The day was filled with phone calls, and I laughed and cried as family and friends remembered Courtney. Noah, David, and Liz sent flowers, Paula, Barb, and Lyann brought flowers, and Judy sent a beautiful keychain and a book called *Mourning has Broken*.

The day after was donation day at Crossroads. I received an email from Donna saying Fox 10 news was going to do a live feed. I was thrilled and excited. Starting out at 4 am in the morning, I got ready and wore the Purse-Impressions t-shirt my sister had made for me. Always promote the brand!!

When we arrived at Crossroads, they informed me Channel 15 had shown up and was going to do a taped interview. Lyann and Rich arrived hauling Ikea bags they had picked up on Wednesday.

I did the taped interview and the live one with Fox. I felt good, and accomplished, and that Courtney was with me the whole time.

Today, Donna from Crossroads gave me a box full of jewelry. I felt compelled to peek inside to see what we got. It was mostly costume type stuff, and I was thinking, "I wonder if I'll find anything good that I would want." LOL! I was also thinking how cute these items would be in the purses.

Then, I opened a box and saw a heart, thinking, "I like hearts." I looked closer. I knew this was a sign from Courtney.

Etched into the heart was the word "MOM."

EPILOGUE

During the Covid summer of 2020, Christie and I traveled for 50 days in our RV. We went to see friends and family and spent time with our three grandchildren.

It was a weird summer as everything was closed. We had to wear masks everywhere, and the vaccine had not yet been approved.

I missed Courtney, as I always do and will, but I was proud of how the charity had flourished and the number of lives we were touching. Her idea was not only working, but it was also making a difference.

I began to receive notes from graduates, both women and men, expressing their gratitude and saying how much the gift and Courtney's story meant to them.

There was only one thing missing, a proper space to run the charity out of. My house could no longer accommodate the amount of inventory that needed to be stored.

During the RV trip, I came up with the 'brilliant' idea of opening a boutique instead of renting a storage space; a place where I could work the charity out of the back and sell purses up front to help support the cause.

The downside of the idea was that we were in the middle of a pandemic, and it might not be the best time to open a business. I ran the concept by my husband and the board, and surprisingly, everyone was supportive. My husband offered to donate some startup money and told me he'd "have my back for rent" if I needed it.

When I asked Nadia her opinion, she gave me the best response, "What do you have to lose? If you don't sell anything then you just overpaid for storage." That's what best friends are for; to assure you that you are not crazy and to go for it.

I found a place in my hometown of Cave Creek, and in September of 2020, I signed a lease. My sister flew out to help me get set up, and I also received help from my husband and Rich L., who painted and put up the shelving.

The boutique has become not only a place where you can shop for purses and jewelry, but also a place to tell Courtney's story; a magical environment where everyone who comes in shares their stories.

Shared are the stories of loss, alcoholism, substance abuse, and suicide. It's a safe place to speak openly about topics that, until the boutique, had been kept to themselves. Many tears have flowed, and we always have Kleenex™ available.

On the bright side, the boutique has become "The Sisterhood of the Traveling Purse." Each purse donation has a story, and each purse sold brings happiness and joy to its new owners.

After rent and expenses are paid, the remaining money is used to buy items to fill the purses we donate. By the summer of 2021, just two years after Courtney's Angel-versary, Purse-Impressions Charity Boutique had donated 2,200 purses and backpacks!

We have added a fifth chapter location in the VA/ Washington DC area started by our good friends, Brian and James. We also added a special new facility to the program in Arizona that helps the Native American community.

Our goal is to add more chapter locations, continue with the boutique, and hope this book expands our overall reach.

If you would like to make a monetary, purse, or product donation, open a chapter, or volunteer your time, please contact us.

My email is Patricia@Purse-Impressions.com

Our website is www.Purse-Impressions.com

On behalf of Courtney and myself, thank you to everyone who has helped me through this journey. God bless you and love you all,

Patricia (MOM)

Purse-Impressions Charity Boutique

POP UP FUNDRAISER

202 Courtney M.

ABOUT THE AUTHORS

Patricia Brusha has spent her career as a successful entrepreneur, speaker, and author in the fields of hospitality, digital marketing, educational conferences, and non-profit organizations. She is also a grateful recovering alcoholic. *Courtney M* is her second published book and first work of non-fiction.

In 2019, Patricia founded Purse-Impressions Charity Boutique in her daughter's memory. Based on an idea conceived by her daughter, Courtney, its mission is to provide support to graduates of rehab as they begin their recovery.

Patricia, her husband, and dog reside in Cave Creek, AZ which also serves as the headquarters for the charity and the boutique. Purse-Impressions has five chapters located in Arizona, Colorado, Florida, Washington, DC, and Canada which collectively support eleven rehab facilities with "Courtney's Program."

Courtney Elizabeth Michaels was born January 7, 1991 as a dual citizen of Canada and the USA. Raised outside of Toronto, Courtney was an amazing, beautiful, and charismatic young woman who sincerely cared for the people in her life. She had a habit of reaching out spontaneously to let people know she was thinking of them, cared about how they were doing, and just to tell them she loved them.

Courtney would be proud to know her legacy lives on both through her published journal and the creation of Purse-Impressions. Courtney's idea brought to fruition by her mother, author Patricia Brusha, continues to help rehab graduates step into their new lives with confidence and dignity.

ACKNOWLEDGMENTS

Losing a child is one of the most devasting experiences anyone could ever have. My heart and love go out to all the parents who have lost a child to alcohol or substance abuse; the pain, the grief, and the guilt are overwhelming.

When I started writing *Courtney M.*, I knew it would "take a village!" just as it did when I went through Courtney's final days and the overwhelming grief that continues to dominate my existence to this day.

I want to thank my husband Christie, or Big Daddy, who has been my rock, my comfort, and my biggest supporter through it all. He was there every minute with Courtney, not just at the end but throughout her entire life. He whole-heartedly encouraged me to start the charity, open the boutique, and write my memoir. Additionally, he has been proud of my sobriety. Thank you for being my husband, partner, and soulmate.

It's hard to find the right words to express my appreciation and love for my sister Kathy, my niece Abbie, and my best friend (and sister by heart) Nadia. These three wonderful and important ladies have been my pillars of strength and my emotional support, and I know they all loved Courtney and miss her every day. I could not have survived the tragedy and shock of losing Courtney without their support and love.

I also want to acknowledge "my girls" Celina, Kelsey, and Sam. Thank you for your awesome friendship with Courtney, the laughter you have brought into my life, and the overwhelming comfort you provided during those dark days. I am blessed to be your "other Mother" and am proud to have watched you all grow up into beautiful, caring women. I love you with all my heart.

As lucky as I am to have my girls, I am also blessed to have four men who are, and were, an important part of both my life and Courtney's. I call them my adopted sons: her cousins Matthew, Noah, and David, and her ex-husband, Adam. Thank you for always being there when I needed you.

I want to express my gratitude and love for my step-children, Beau and Lea, who Courtney loved having as her siblings and who brought wonderful grandchildren into our lives.

I also want to thank all my friends and family who were right there with me through my darkest days.

A very special thank you to my editor, Dr. Alisa Cooper, who took such special care to honor Courtney's words and keep her voice intact. She is a phenomenal woman, and I was blessed to find her, as well as my publisher, Patricia Brooks, and my book designer, Caren Cantrell, who have all brought this most personal project to life.

Finally, I want to acknowledge those fighting addiction and their families. Stay strong, stay positive, you can do this! I hope Courtney's story inspires you to pause and appreciate that not only is there life outside of addiction but a wonderful, happy, and fulfilling life in recovery.

In these 5 minutes, everything is okay!